Valentine School Parties

What Do I Do?™

AWARD WINNING AUTHOR

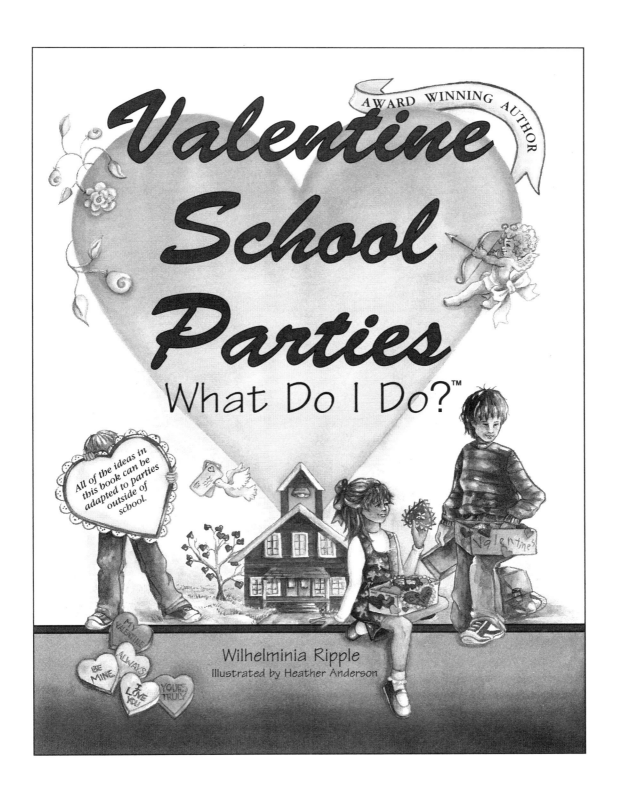

All of the ideas in this book can be adapted to parties outside of school.

Wilhelminia Ripple

Illustrated by Heather Anderson

Valentine School Parties...What Do I Do?™ Author Wilhelminia Ripple

Text and Illustration Copyright© 1998 by Wilhelminia Ripple. All rights reserved. No part of this book may be reproduced or transmitted in any means, electronic or mechanical, including photocopying, recording, or stored in a data base or retrieval system except where noted in the text and in the case of brief passages to be used for reviews. To get permission please contact Oakbrook Publishing House.

Printed and bound in the United States of America.

Printing 10 9 8 7 6 5 4 3 2 1

Publisher's Cataloging-in-Publication
(Provided by Quality Books, Inc.)

Ripple, Wilhelminia.
    Valentine school parties : what do I do? / Wilhelminia
Ripple ; illustrated by Heather Anderson ; editor Dianne
Lorang. -- 1st ed.
    p. cm. -- (What do I do? ; #2)
    Includes index.
    Preassigned LCCN: 98-91455
    ISBN 0-9649939-9-6

    1. Children's parties. 2. Valentine's Day. 3. Games.
4. Education, Elementary -- Parent participation.   I. Title.

GV1205.R57 1998   793.2'1
                         QBI98-696

To order:
1-888-738-1733

Oakbrook Publishing House
P.O. Box 2463
Littleton, Colorado 80161-2463
(303) 738-1733 • FAX: (303) 797-1995
Or email us at: Oakbrook@whatdoidobooks.com
Website: http://www.whatdoidobooks.com

This Book is
Happily Dedicated

To the family and friends of
Kimberly Anne Hill.
May their hearts -♥-
always have room for her.

To my husband Mark
and
To my children Mark, Nick, and Michelle
for their ongoing support
and
To all who believed in me!

Acknowledgments

Thank you to my family and friends who helped me in so many ways.

Special thanks to the children, teachers, and parents who allowed me to interview them:
Carla Alley, Lila Arnold, Melonie Ayers, Sean Ayers, Theresa Ayers, Nancy Brasfield, Linda Brown, Tracy Bryson, Kathy Callaway, Sandy Camp, Doreen Carlson, Jackie Cooper, Kaylyn Cooper, Travis Cooper, Leslie Csikos, Tani Eley, Tommy Jo Epley, Mrs. Gamboa, Gail Hill, Kelly Hill, Jackie Jacobs, Stephanie Major, Cassie Mason, Lisa Moffatt, Leslie McCarthy, Samantha McCarthy, Tamara Osburn, Alyssa Ripple, Priscilla Ripple, Adam Rowan, Dana Rowan, Andrew Schildkret, Joan Schildkret, Chris Schleig, Christine Stanislawski, Alberta Shellem, Jill Stephens, Linda Stephens, Gae Jean Taylor, Rob Taylor, and Judi Thielen.

Special thanks to those who judged our Valentine Container Contest:
Jill Day, Lou Ikard, Donna Kortman, Julie Krohn, and Gwen Rosentrater.

Special thanks to the children who allowed me to share their Valentine containers with all of you:
Brook Alessandrini, Alex, Kelsey Antun, Pat Botkins, Wade Brown, Alison Cavanaugh, Steven Christiansen, Thomas Christiansen, Matthew Cloyd, Taylor Craver, Katie Day, Nathan Finneman, Kalyn Fong, Jessica Gallegos, Rachel Goold, Scott Heldt, Erin Johnson and her dad, Judi Krew and Travis, Allison Pelissier, Michelle Ripple, Tyler Sales and John Christiansen, Kayla Schaecher, Kelsey Schaecher, Holly Simpson, Lynette Simpson, Spencer Vore, and Clayton Wilbanks.

Special thanks to those who helped in different ways:
Dolores Arcuri, Dominick Arcuri, Ben Blea, Tammy Brenner, Denise Campuzano, Colorado Independent Publisher Association (CIPA), Nancy Ecker, Paula Farney, Bridgid Hendricks, Joanne Hill, Mark Hopkins Elementary, Barb Johnson, Pam & Jeff Kortman, Becky Leon, Rachelle Lifpitz, Rose Mason, Karlyn McCrumb, Publishers Marketing Association (PMA), Ralph Moody Elementary, Room Parents of Littleton Colorado, Sauder Elementary, Gloria Schwiesow, Laura Sexson, Karen Simpson, The United States Postal Service Littleton Branch, and Laura Ingalls Wilder Elementary.

Special thanks to my reviewers:
Monica Lobser, Tammy Robbins, Lauren Sicking, Kathy Totten, and Nancy Weinberger.

Special thanks to Karen Timm for her Valentine poems.

Special thanks to the following who were patient in working with me:
      Cover Designer - Bobbi Shupe of E.P. Puffin & Company
      Editor - Dianne Lorang of The Write Help
      Illustrator - Heather Anderson
      Graphic Artists - Jennifer Franson and Cheri Pomeroy
      Production Assistants - Brian Doll and Lindsay Junkin
      Production Coordinator - Vonda Wall

And if I have forgotten you "Thank You!"

About the Author
Wilhelminia "Willie" Ripple is the award-winning author of *Halloween School Parties ... What Do I Do?*™ She has 10 years of experience in collecting and creating party ideas. Willie currently lives in Colorado with her husband Mark, and their three children.

CHAPTER 2

TABLE OF CONTENTS

SECRET VALENTINE HANDSHAKE
By Michelle Ripple

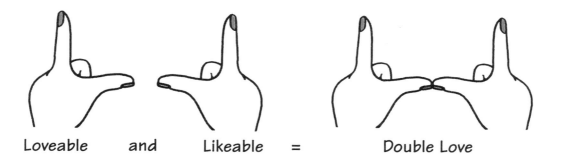

Loveable   and   Likeable   =   Double Love

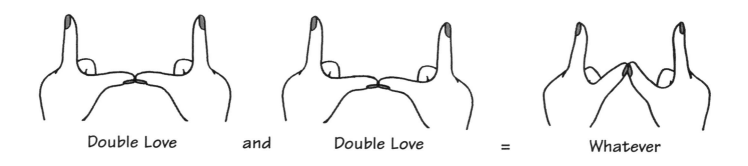

Double Love   and   Double Love   =   Whatever

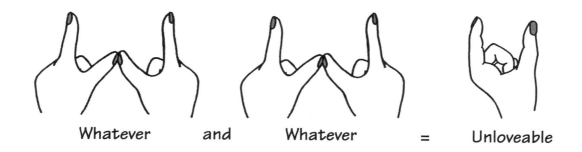

Whatever   and   Whatever   =   Unloveable

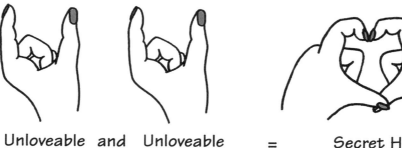

Unloveable   and   Unloveable   =   Secret Heart

8

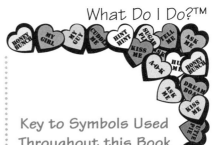

INTRODUCTION
How To Use This Book

Valentine School Parties...What Do I Do?™ will help you plan successful and fun Valentine classroom parties for kindergartners through sixth graders. These ideas can also be adapted to Valentine parties outside of school, as well as to a broader age group. This book contains six how-to chapters, including one-of-a-kind information about all aspects of room parenting. The chapters include The What, Why, and How of Room Parenting, Games, Hearts, Crafts & Favors, Sweets, Drinks, and Valentine Boxes. Within minutes, your party will be planned. No more fussing, no more headaches. It couldn't be easier.

First, start with a theme. There are six to choose from — Hearts, Cupids, Post Office, Love & Friendship, Animals, and February & Presidents. Now you have direction. Creating a party becomes fun and easy, and your party will look so well put together that everyone will be impressed. Let's say you choose Hearts. The minute you walk into a store, your eyes automatically zero in on heart-related items, such as heart plates, napkins, cups, and favors. If you hear or read elsewhere about party ideas that don't relate to your theme, put them into a folder for next year or the year after. However, some of the best parties can be those where themes are combined.

After choosing a theme, pick games related to it from Chapter Two. Find ones appropriate for your grade level. Most of the games can be played in five minutes. Feel free to adapt them to fit your needs — be creative. Remember, all kids love prizes. Be aware that it causes confusion for children to put their prizes in their desks or backpacks. I try to give ones that can be worn, such as Valentine stickers or ink stamps for their faces or hands. Necklaces and rings work well, but are primarily for girls. Buttons are appropriate for both genders. Candy is a great prize, if eaten right away and the children aren't running around. If you have chosen larger prizes, show them the prize and have it waiting for them in a favor bag or at their desk.

Next, move on to the Hearts, Crafts & Favors chapter. Choose a craft that kids can make during the party, or get some parents together to make crafts for the kids (I like the assembly line approach). This can be quite fun for parents. The all-time favorite craft is Smooshies on Page 101. Be sure to make them once during your career as a party mom or dad. There are also plenty of store-bought favors you can buy if you'll be short on time or manpower — but shop early for the best ones.

Finally, no party is complete without refreshments. Be the talk of the school with unique ones from the Sweets and Drink chapters, where you will find plenty of fast and easy recipes (be sure to read the small introduction about drinks at the beginning of Chapter 5). Choose sweets that match your theme, and plan on serving two sweets — one is not enough. Valentines can be exchanged and opened by the children while they are eating. This works quite well. And always refer to the sweets and drinks by their cute Valentine names — they taste better that way.

Be sure to check out the last chapter full of award-winning Valentine boxes, which will help you and your child have a fun and entertaining time together — or just to give your children ideas for boxes they can make for their Valentine parties. Don't forget to share these ideas with the teacher for a classroom project, or even with other parents.

So remember, choose a theme — it's the start of any successful party — then go from there. This book is written so you can quickly go from chapter to chapter to create a memorable party. Remember, no more fussing, no more headaches. It couldn't be easier.

What Do I Do?™

Key to Symbols Used Throughout this Book

Knowledge Symbol
Educational facts relating to themes to share with the children.

Favorite Symbol
Don't miss this game (craft, sweet, etc.)

Messy Symbol
Sure to cause dirty hands or faces: have paper towels ready.

Supply Symbol
Complete list of needed items, for each game, craft, sweet, treat, etc.

Envelope Symbol
Easy to copy, complete list of all ingredients/ supplies needed for each section.

Note: Throughout the book, we will refer to both genders as "he" for the sake of consistency. "He" can be a girl or a boy.

9

CHAPTER ONE
THE WHAT, WHY, AND HOW OF ROOM PARENTING

WHAT IS A ROOM PARENT?

There are many definitions for the term "room parent." I guess the technical definition is "someone who assists the teacher in various ways." As a room parent, you might help the teacher in the classroom with cutting, pasting, making copies, organizing book orders, assisting on field trips, reading stories, baking, etc. The list varies for each school.

The purpose of this book is to help you, the room parent, in another area that is often your responsibility — classroom party planning. At my childrens' school, some room parents who wanted only to help with school parties were confused by the title "room parents," so we decided to call these parents "party planners." Therefore, our party planners' only purpose is to plan parties for the school year, and it is our room parents' responsibility to help the teachers in other ways. But for the sake of not confusing you, throughout this book the title "room parent" will be used instead of "party planner", since the former is more widely accepted. I also use the word "parent" even though a room parent may be a grandparent, uncle, aunt, friend, neighbor, or community member.

WHAT IS A ROOM PARTY?

A "room party" is held at school during school time. Many schools hold these parties the last hour of the day, but some schools are finding that the first hour of the day works well. School administrators feel that the kids focus better for the day if they get the party over with early. Each class has its own party, usually held in its classroom. A typical party consists of playing games and having refreshments, as well as taking home favors and/or making a craft. Although the parents throw the party, the teacher usually stays.

This book focuses on Valentine's Day parties. However, other common parties at schools can include Christmas/Hanukkah or Winter parties, Easter or Spring parties, and Halloween parties, which I covered in my first book, *Halloween School Parties...What Do I Do?*™ The most popular parties for schools to hold, however, are Halloween and Valentine's Day.

HOW DO YOU BECOME A ROOM PARENT?

You can usually sign up at back-to-school night or curriculum night at the beginning of the school year. Some schools might also send home a volunteer sign-up package during the first few weeks of school. Every school will be different, so check with your child's teacher, especially if you are new to the school. Also, check to see what's expected of you before you sign-up. If you only want to help with a specific event such as the Valentine's Day party, but your school's room parents do more, then write that on the sign-up sheet. But please don't hesitate to volunteer even if work or other circumstances limit what you can do. If you can't attend a classroom party or help plan the event, why not offer to donate materials or bake goodies? Keep in mind that you should always let the head room parent know your plans — many room parents have complained that the "surprise" snacks/goodies dropped off are more of a hindrance than a help.

Once everyone signs up, a head room parent needs to be chosen. Your teacher, room parent coordinator, or Parent Teacher Organization (PTO) might do the choosing. (In some schools, the parent-teacher support group is called the Parent Teacher Association (PTA), the Parent Teacher Student Association (PTSA), or the Parent Association (PA). Throughout this book we will use the term PTO.) Sometimes two or three parents in the same class want to be the

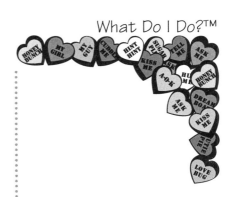

head room parent: Other times, no one volunteers. When the latter happens, the teacher may suggest a classroom parent be a head room parent. Typically, when a teacher asks a parent, they will not refuse. At our school our sign-up sheet asks if you would like to be a head room parent. You then check "yes," "no," or "if no one else will." Many times, I will call whoever checked "if no one else will" and find a head room parent. Some schools ask several parents to work together, or assign one parent to be head room parent for one party and another to handle the other party. This works great, as long as the teacher(s), parents, and coordinator know! There can never be too many room parents. (Well, almost never – Kindergarten classes can have an overwhelming number of room parents.) Usually, however, the more help, the less work there is for everyone, and the better the party is for the kids.

WHY SHOULD YOU BE A ROOM PARENT?

1. Because you are needed!

2. It's one more step to being a better parent.

3. It keeps you in tune with how your child acts in school.

4. Children whose parents volunteer at school tend to do better overall.

5. Children learn what they see; it's important for our kids to see us helping out.

6. Not only do your children appreciate you, but the teacher, the school, and the other children do, too.

7. Being around children at school will make you feel young again.

8. You might revive some lost creativity.

9. You gain valuable experience from teamwork.

10. It's a great opportunity to make friends.

WHAT IS A HEAD ROOM PARENT?

Each class usually has a head room parent whose main purpose is to be a contact person that can be reached by other room parents, teachers, and the PTO. The head room parent's job can include but is not limited to:

1. Calling other room parents to plan the party.

2. Collecting and distributing class party money.

3. Making decisions when and if needed.

4. Communicating with the teacher, PTO, school administration, etc.

5. Turning in a record of volunteer hours to the PTO or the school district.

Your school will let you know what your responsibilities are.

When your children are grown up and you will no longer be a room parent, what do you hope to remember about your room parent experience?

"The twinkle in my son's eyes, the smile one his face, and his excitement at every party. I'll never forget it!"

Carla Alley
Kearney, Missouri

"I will remember spending some special time with my kids on their turf (classroom). I will also remember seeing all the crazy antics of the other kids that were a part of my children's daily lives."

Dana Rowan
Libertyville, Illinois

"Pleasant memories of kids' smiles."

Linda Stephens
Mineral Wells, West Virginia

HELP FOR THE HEAD ROOM PARENT

You have been selected as head room parent for your child's class. Congratulations! Here are some helpful tips:

At least three, sometimes four weeks before the party, call and meet with your other room parents (who could be moms, dads, grandmas, grandpas, aunts, uncles, and legal guardians — don't refuse anybody or any help).

Caution: Assignments given to some helpers can get lost or forgotten if you start too soon. But keep in mind that a lot of room parents get nervous if they are not called at least two weeks before the party. What might work better would be to call room parents four weeks prior to the party, but schedule a meeting three weeks before.

Before your meeting, communicate with the classroom teacher either by talking on the phone, sending a note with questions or catching the teacher at a break such as recess, lunch, or after school. Some teachers will tell you at back-to-school night or curriculum night how they want to be contacted: If not, ask them. Allow a week for the teacher to return your note. Most return it in a day, but you may have to wait longer and even gently remind some teachers. I have found that most teachers prefer a note because they can answer my questions at their convenience, right on the note paper, then send it back to me. I can then keep the note for future reference. Here are some questions for the teacher that will help you plan your party:

1. How many children are in the class? Boys? Girls? Correct spelling of names?

2. Are there any new students since the beginning of the year? Or have any students left since the last party?

3. Are there any children with physical disabilities?

4. Do you prefer the children to eat when the party first starts or at the end of the party?

5. Does anybody, including the teacher, have food allergies? **This is very important!**

6. Do you have any preferences for games, food, favors, crafts, etc.?

7. Do you want the children to open Valentines during party time? How much time should we allow?

8. Is it okay to set up in the room before the party begins?

9. Can the desks and chairs be rearranged?

10. How do you like to handle younger siblings coming to the party? (See the Teacher Thought Page.)

11. What time should the party start and end? (This information might be given to you by the room parent coordinator.)

Setting up the room during a recess or lunch break can work well if the party immediately follows. Try to bring in the supplies early in the morning before school starts. Once the supplies are in the room, setting them up in the right areas usually takes no more than five minutes. Whatever method you use, avoid interrupting the class. No matter how quiet you are, the kids will stop what they are doing and wave or say "Hi!" They are curious, excited, and want to know what's going on. Some teachers do not appreciate this distraction. Here is one final question to ask teachers of older children (grades five and six): Is it okay to combine other classes from the same level for one huge party in the gym, or outside if the weather permits?

After being a head room parent, what suggestions can you pass along to others who will become the head room parents?

"Surround yourself with willing, dependable helpers."

Tracy Bryson
Plano, Texas

"Communication, communication, communication."

Melonie Ayers
Toledo, Ohio

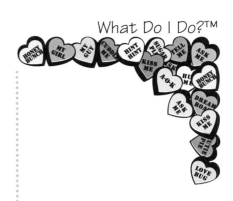

The next step after calling all your room parents and scheduling a meeting is to think about what the meeting should cover and then jot down an agenda. (What's the main goal? Ideas you have? Order of the meeting? Who should do what?) This way you can get down to business when the time comes. Otherwise, an hour or more can go by very fast without accomplishing anything. This is irritating for many parents who are on a tight schedule. Also, by making it known what time the meeting will end you can help keep it on track. What works well is to give a handout sheet such as the room parent's assignment list which appears on page 21. Everyone can take their own notes to remember what they are responsible for. Have paper and pens on hand for those who did not bring any.

It is fun to make a little party out of this first planning meeting. I like to serve refreshments, usually something simple like Valentine cookies and punch. If you serve your refreshments with Valentine paper goods, it helps get the parents in the party mood. They will be surprised and pleased by your extra touches.

As a head room parent, you may also opt for a meeting at a restaurant or at school to avoid serving refreshments and/or cleaning your house. Plus, the meeting will seem more business-like. If you choose to meet at school, ask your PTO or school office where you can meet, and whether your meeting time is okay in that location. Remember to keep down the noise and encourage younger children not to run around.

If the meeting is at your house, it helps not to seat children at the table where you will be working. Plan an area where any young visitors can play within sight of their parents. Put toys out or put a video into the VCR. A meeting without children would be ideal but isn't always possible. My experience has shown me that a two-hour meeting is best because there will always be problems such as people arriving late or leaving early.

Caution: Don't assume all is okay when you don't hear from your parent volunteers. Only assume all is okay when you verify party plans with them. Call them a few days before the party (and the night before, if need be) to see if they have done what they said they would do.

CLASS PARTY MONEY

At most schools, money is collected from each student to be used for class parties. This is usually done at the beginning of the school year. Collections can vary from $2 to $10 for the school year (some schools collect no money and only ask for donations from parents). That amount is divided between the number of parties. For example, at a school where there are two parties — Valentine's Day and Halloween — $2 might be collected from each student ($1 per student per party). If a class has 25 students, it will collect $50 in party money if each student pays. Each school handles the collection and distribution of the money the way it thinks best.

Some schools collect the money by way of the classroom teachers who turn it into the school office. Then it is given to the PTO, which distributes the money to the head room parents. Money for the Valentine's Day party usually is given to the head room parents in January, whereas September is the usual time to distribute money for the Halloween party.

There are two ways in which PTOs generally handle party money. First, they may choose not to distribute the money to head room parents, but instead to buy bulk favors, drinks, and napkins, etc., for the whole school. This may be done to treat all classes equally. Room parents would still plan all the games, crafts, activities, and food for their individual classrooms, but would have no class money to work with. In this situation, you need to get donations.

How does your school handle party money?

"No school party money — strictly donations."

Stephanie Major
Franktown, Colorado

"The PTA donates $3.00 per child for the year — parents are asked to donate $2.00. This gives us $5.00 per child to work with."

Doreen Carlson
Minnetonka, Minnesota

If you are or were a coordinator/chair person, do you have any quick tips to share with room parents?

"Try to be over-organized. Beforehand, I make a list of every activity we are going to do and then mentally imagine myself going through each one. As I do this, I list everything I could possibly need (for example, tape to put on the floor as a starting line for games). Then I make sure I have everything ahead of time. I also contact parents ahead of time to get someone to be in charge of each activity that we're going to be doing. I always make a sheet for each station that includes: 1) the rules of the activity, 2) the items to be used, 3) a diagram of how everything is to be set up, and 4) prizes to be given."

Carla Alley
Kearney, Missouri

"If you find or hear of a good game or craft but it doesn't seem feasible for a large group, with a little thought and ingenuity, anything can be 'doctored' for your specific needs."

Dana Rowan
Libertyville, Illinois

"If you are helping, help all of the children, not only yours."

Joan Schildkret
Highlands Ranch, Colorado

Some parents feel that they donate enough through school fundraisers and the giving of their time. So be as careful as possible when asking for party donations. Ask your PTO for suggestions if needed.

Second, the PTO may collect the money from all the classes and divide that amount per student to obtain a per-student figure. For example, if you have 450 students and receive $2 per student, you will have $900. But if all the money hasn't been collected, the per-student figure will be less than $2. Let's say you only received $810 — you would still divide that amount by 450 students, This would give you $1.80 per student to divide between two parties — or $.90 per student per party. You would then multiply $.90 times the number of students in each class to determine the total amount for each classroom per party. For example, if there are 20 students in a class, that class would receive $18 for the Valentine's Day party and the same amount for the Halloween party. This per-student method of allocating party money may vary somewhat from school to school. At some schools, for example, if there is a shortfall, the PTO may choose to make up the difference in order to ensure $2 per student. Also, some schools might have a budget for needy families if this is where the shortfall comes from. Any questions regarding party money should be directed to the proper source. This might be the principal or the PTO. Check with your child's teacher.

WHAT IS A ROOM PARENT COORDINATOR?

Each school usually has a room parent coordinator or party chairperson whose job is to find head room parents for each class, train them if necessary, distribute money, communicate with the PTO/school, and solve any problems which might arise. The PTO/school is very happy for anyone to volunteer for this position. Once you do this for a year, it's quite easy to be the coordinator another year and the following years after that. You will need to be a good leader, and enthusiastic. Also, creativity is a plus.

QUICK TIPS FOR THE ROOM PARENT COORDINATOR/CHAIRPERSON

1. Get someone to help with the coordinator job if at all possible. You may want help with the phone-calling, making ideas for an example table at a meeting, getting money ready, and/or reporting back to the PTO/school.

2. If your job is to choose who the head room parents will be in each class, choose the most enthusiastic, energized parents. *Note:* A working parent might be a better choice than a stay-at-home mom if she is organized, creative, willing, and know how to get a job done.

3. Plan a meeting for room parents (especially head room parents) a month before the Valentine's Day party. Because some schools will just be getting back from winter break, you might want to send home a notice about the meeting before the break and once again after the break. Have example tables with plenty of ideas for crafts/favors, treats and games. (Room parents find this especially helpful.) Hand out any party information and class party money at this time. Our school likes to have head room parents sign for the money.

4. At the meeting, give each head room parent the party report form on page 20. Ask that the form be filled out and sent back to you in care of the school. Give them about one week to do this. Collect receipts with the form if needed for the PTO. This form can be quite helpful for future use.

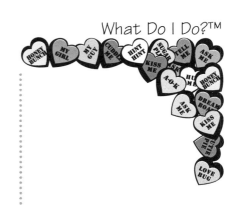

5. To ensure all parties are successful, call all head room mothers about a week before the party. Ask them to tell you a little bit about their party. This is when a lot of room parents ask for help with planning their party (especially games). Suggest quick and easy ideas, because time is running out. Also, ask how they are doing with the budget.

6. For future use, keep a folder with the following information:
   a. Names and phone numbers of all room parents.
   b. All party report forms.
   c. Any party information handed out.
   d. Any notes you took while corresponding with your head room parents.

7. Your leadership skills will greatly improve with this job, but remember — have fun!

HELPFUL HINTS FOR ROOM PARENTS

1. Communicate!

2. Physical education teachers, music teachers, librarians, secretaries, custodians, special education teachers, and the principal are usually forgotten as potential classroom helpers at party time. They are good resources for you if you do not have enough parent volunteer help for the day. You can even plan extra sweets and drinks for them. (If you have a lot of extra refreshments, you may want to set them in the teachers' lounge for everyone to enjoy.)

3. A room parent may have more than one child attending the school. They need to be aware that it is very difficult for other room helpers if they party hop. This problem can be solved by going to Sam's Valentine's Day party and Vince's Halloween party. If a mother has more than two children at the school, maybe the father can help by attending one of the other children's parties.

4. Purchase or make extra favors because some may break or new students may have joined the class.

5. Make sure you have an updated class list.

6. Check with the teacher on the correct spelling of names if you are personalizing anything.

7. Ask the teacher if younger siblings can come to the parties. If the teacher okays this, ask your room parents to include extra sweets, drinks, and favors for them. Always include sweets and drinks for the teacher(s) and parent helpers. Favors for the teacher(s) would also be nice. They can give them to their children or save them for students who lose theirs.

8. Keep in contact with the teacher about all party plans, including food.

9. If trying a new game, practice it first at home, but try to keep it and all plans a secret from your child who will be attending the party. He will enjoy the party more that way.

10. Have everything ready the night before the party.

11. Don't forget your camera, film, and/or video recorder.

12. Make nametags for the room parents as well as for the children. For younger grades it works well to write "Tammy's Mom," and "Dom's Dad" on the tags. For older grades, it is appropriate to write out the parent's last name, for example, "Mrs. Arcuri."

13. Depending how much needs to be unloaded from your car and what the weather is like, get to the party one-half to one hour early. Bring everything as close to the classroom as possible without disrupting anyone.

14. Meet party helpers approximately 15 minutes before the party starts, to go over party plans.

15. Kids can draw numbers or straws to decide who starts.

16. Dividing the class into smaller groups works best for rotating stations to play games or make crafts. I have found that four groups work well in any class size.

Do you have any tips for room parents?

"Be organized, delegate, and relax."

Alberta Shellem
Baltimore, Maryland

"KISS - Keep It Simple Sweetie!!"
Leslie McCarthy
Littleton, Colorado

"Get favors in advance or they are hard to find."
Anonymous

"Be involved now while your children want your love and attention."
Christine Stanislawski
Littleton, Colorado

"STAY CALM!"
Gae Jean Taylor
Littleton, Colorado

"Your job is most important because what you do affects the children. Be on time and include parents. I send a note home before every party informing the parents when the party will be and ask them to please come. I let them know that they're always welcome. I also try to plan party favors that will be kept and not thrown out."
Kathy Callaway
Wichita Falls, Texas

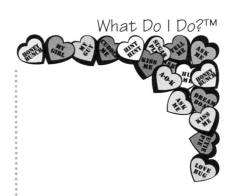

17. Boys versus girls works great in fourth through sixth grades.

18. A good way to divide kids into rotating groups is to give them nametags based on the party's combination of themes. Another great idea for dividing kids into groups is to give them playing cards (the heart suit of course). Pre-cut each of the 13 cards into two pieces and place in a Valentine container. (You will have 26 card halves minus the Jokers. Use an additional card deck for a larger class or adjust the cards accordingly for a smaller class). Each child chooses one. Then he finds his match and goes to the group that corresponds to that card. For example, if a child chooses a Jack, he finds the other Jack, and the two children go to the group of Jacks, Queens and Kings. Another group can be the 1, 2, 3's and so on. Decide which numbers go into which groups ahead of time, and designate areas where they will meet. Keep in mind that you will want to keep the groups as equal as possible.

19. A Valentine activity on paper, such as a crossword puzzle, works well as a back-up for children who run out of things to do or who are waiting to take turns at a particular game. (Don't have too much waiting time as kids are always ready to go.)

20. Give prizes to all the kids.

21. Start and end the party on time.

22. For easier clean-up, bring a large plastic garbage bag to the party. The bag will eliminate overflowing trash cans, and the custodians will love you. It also helps to have a roll of paper towels or a sponge for spills, which we know will happen. Most classrooms have sinks for your use.

23. For more hints, read all the helpful hints which you will find before each chapter.

24. Be a room parent next year. Better yet, be a head room parent or a room parent coordinator.

25. Have fun!

Do you remember making Valentine boxes in school? Tell us about it.

"We usually made ours at home and you could do anything you wanted. Then at the party, a panel of judges came around to each room and selected the top 3 boxes. We got our picture taken with our boxes and they were published in the yearbook."
Carla Alley
Kearney, Missouri

"We made Valentine boxes at school which my kids have never done — sort of dissapointing."
Stephanie Major
Franktown, Colorado

"Yes it was fun being creative and cutting out hearts."
Judi Thielen
Ellicott City, Maryland

Valentine School Parties

NOTES

PARTY REPORT FORM

Party Date & Time: _____

Teacher & Grade: _____

Head Room Parent: _____

Budget: _____

How much spent: _____

How much left: _____

Refreshments served:

Sweets: 1. _____ **Drinks:** 1. _____

2. _____ 2. _____

Games or Craft Activities (Briefly describe, include prizes if any.)

1. _____
   _____

2. _____
   _____

3. _____
   _____

4. _____
   _____

5. _____
   _____

6. _____
   _____

Take-Home Favors (Briefly describe):

1. _____
2. _____
3. _____
4. _____
5. _____
6. _____

What Worked: _____

What Didn't Work: _____

How Many Parents Attended: _____

Please return to the Room Parent Coordinator or PTO box within one week of the party. Thank you!

ROOM PARENT'S ASSIGNMENT LIST

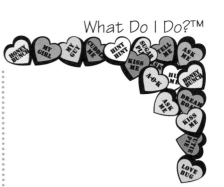

What Do I Do?™

NOTES

Party Date & Time: _____

Teacher & Grade: _____

Head Room Parent: _____

Budget: _____

Teacher Suggestions: _____

Responsibilities:	**Room Parent Helpers:**
Set-Up	_____
Clean-Up	_____
Nametags	_____
First Sweet	_____
Second Sweet	_____
Plasticware	_____
Napkins	_____
Plates	_____
Drinks	_____
Cups	_____
Punch Bowl	_____
Ice	_____

Take-Home Favors:	**Room Parent Helpers:**
1. _____	1. _____
2. _____	2. _____
3. _____	3. _____
4. _____	4. _____
5. _____	5. _____
6. _____	6. _____

Games or Craft Activities & Prizes:	**Room Parent Helpers:**
1. _____	1. _____
2. _____	2. _____
3. _____	3. _____
4. _____	4. _____
5. _____	5. _____
6. _____	6. _____

TEACHERS, TELL US

What suggestions do you have for a great Valentine's party?

"Open Valentines first and then put them away. This way they will not be lost during the party. Kindergartners should not address their Valentines, it will be easier for them to pass them out."

Linda Brown
O'Fallon, Missouri

"Not telling the kids ahead of time, HA! I suggest games, songs, refreshments, cupcakes or cookies (no cake, it's too messy), and opening Valentines."

Sandy Camp
Wichita Falls, Texas

"I love to have a 'Valentine Lunch Auction.' The children decorate a bag at home (gift bag, brown bag, etc.) with a Valentine theme (hearts, etc.). They are given guidelines for what they can put in a healthy lunch and pack it in their bag. The bags come to school 'undercover,' hidden from others, until the auction begins. To buy a lunch, they use money they've earned during the week by accomplishing tasks. Then the auction begins! The children bid on the bag they like (not knowing the contents) with the money they've worked hard to earn!"

Lisa Moffatt
Parker, Colorado

"1) PLAN AHEAD - have everything ready for crafts, games, and food so the kids aren't kept waiting, 2) plan more activities than you think you'll need, and 3) use a mix of crafts, games and snacks and end with opening Valentine cards."

Linda Stephens
Mineral Wells, West Virginia

"A great party is a well organized one. Planning and having everything ready will make it flow and be great. You also need games, music, food, and great moms as volunteers."

Mrs. Gamboa
Wichita Falls, Texas

Do you like room parents to discuss party plans with you or surprise you?

"I like to know what is being planned in case I see a problem that parents might not foresee."

Mrs. Gamboa
Wichita Falls, Texas

"I like surprises!"

Chris Schleig
Canton, Ohio

"I appreciate hearing party plans in advance so I can provide needed classroom materials or make suggestions. Sometimes students have special diets, allergies, etc."

Linda Stephens
Mineral Wells, West Virginia

Do your students make Valentine boxes in class or out of class? Why?

"We make our boxes in class prior to the Valentine party so that the children have time to enjoy delivering their own cards. They also take turns wearing the mailman hat and letter bag."

Linda Stephens
Mineral Wells, West Virginia

"In class, so that we can share ideas and learn from each other's creativity."

Mrs. Gamboa
Wichita Falls, Texas

"I'd rather have the Valentine boxes look similar so we make heart folders in class. I find that many times, projects done at home are not done by the children but rather by their parents."

Tani Eley
Franktown, Colorado

Do you like morning or afternoon parties? Why?

"Afternoon – stir them up and send them home!"

Tommy Jo Epley
Wichita Falls, Texas

"Afternoon, because it's hard to get their attention after a party."

Jackie Jacobs
Wichita Falls, Texas

"I prefer afternoon parties. The children are usually too tired or excited to do school work after a party."

Tamara Osburn
Canton Ohio

22

YOUR THOUGHTS

What Do I Do?™

What thoughts do you have on younger siblings coming to the school parties?

"I don't have a problem with it as long as they're supervised and they've been included in the our activity count so that they can be an active participant."

Tani Eley
Franktown, Colorado

"I think that they shouldn't attend since it is a special time for their brother or sister. They should wait and anticipate the excitement when they get in school."

Gail Hill
Wichita Falls, Texas

"As a teacher of young children, I prefer that younger siblings not attend. It is very difficult for young students to understand why they must follow classroom rules (stay seated, speak quietly, etc.) if toddlers are allowed to roam freely around the classroom. We encourage parents to take turns staying home with younger siblings so they can each attend some of the parties. Also, often there aren't enough treats prepared for extra visitors, which can lead to hurt feelings."

Linda Stephens
Mineral Wells, West Virginia

Tell us about your best room party.

"The children were divided into five groups. They spent about 5 to 7 minutes at each of the activities organized by a mom. Then they ate, it was great fun!"

Chris Schleig
Canton, Ohio

"My best Valentine's Day Party was very organized. There were a variety of activities planned. The room mothers all knew what they were responsible for. It was fun for all."

Tamara Osburn
Canton, Ohio

"Our students shared something about love and they made a Valentine for a loved one."

Jackie Jacobs
Wichita Falls, Texas

"The best ones are organized with games and refreshments. Also, our PTA usually gives the kids some cute memento."

Nancy Brasfield
Wichita Falls, Texas

What percentage of children add items inside their Valentine cards? What kind of items?

"50% add small wrapped candies."

Nancy Brasfield
Wichita Falls, Texas

"40% add pencils, gum, erasers, and candy. They also enjoy cards that fold into paper airplanes and dolls."

Sandy Camp
Wichita Falls, Texas

"25% add candy. They also like stickers."

Tani Eley
Franktown, Colorado

"40% add gum and candy. Kids enjoy food items more than objects."

Mrs. Gamboa
Wichita Falls, Texas

"10 to 15% add candy. It's candy they like best!"

Chris Schleig
Canton, Ohio

"50% add candy, stickers, pencils, and toys. They are all a big hit."

Tamara Osburn
Canton, Ohio

"30% add Hershey's Kisses®, Valentine candy, suckers, etc. but the kids don't bother to read the Valentines because they're ripping out the candy."

Leslie Csikos
Littleton, Colorado

"25% add candy and stickers."

Linda Brown
O'Fallon, Missouri

When the party is going on, do you mind being a helper when or where needed?

"I usually don't mind helping, but I also like to use that time to be able to talk to my students and get to know them in a different, relaxed setting."

Leslie Csikos
Littleton, Colorado

"I love being a helper. I feel awkward sitting back and watching."

Lila Arnold
Wichita Falls, Texas

"Not at all! I get all kinds of new ideas!"

Tani Eley
Franktown, Colorado

"Not at all! My favorite job, though, is taking pictures."

Sandy Camp
Wichita Falls, Texas

CHAPTER TWO
GAMES

HELPFUL HINTS

HELPFUL HINTS FOR GAMES

1. A rotation of four games at any grade level works best. Keep games short! Five minutes long for young children (Grades K-2) and ten minutes for older children (Grades 3-6).

2. Choose age-appropriate games. Each game in this book is marked with the ideal grade levels. Use your judgement or the teacher's if you think the game can work for the class but isn't marked for your grade level.

3. Keep all directions simple, because children are tired of listening all day long. Party time is party time!

4. Always explain to the children the object of the game, even obvious ones like Tic-Tac-Toe.

5. Have an extra game or two planned just in case you have extra time, or if a game is not working well. An easy game to play at the last minute with no prior work is Red, Red, & More Red (Chapter 2).

6. If you will be playing elimination games, have something for the eliminated children to do. Some suggestions: they can cheer for their friends, be game helpers, or help with the music. You can also have a jar filled with conversation hearts and let the children guess how many candies are in the jar. The closest guess wins the jar of candy.

7. Have one parent at each game station. Have two parents if you need to retrieve anything such as balls or arrows when playing relay games. You will find that the games go smoother and faster when you have that extra parent helping.

8. If you are using rotating stations, one person needs to tell the class when to rotate. They can do this by blowing a whistle or turning the lights on and off. Explain to the parents that they should replay their game until time is up.

9. Masking tape placed on the floor works well for a starting line. Move it closer for younger grades and farther back for older grades.

10. Make adjustments for handicapped children such as moving the starting line up when playing tossing games, or allowing them more time to play.

11. Read the Introduction for information regarding prizes.

12. All children should receive prizes, but to make winners feel special, let them be first in the refreshment line.

13. Remember to keep all games and prizes safe for all children.

14. A parent can be preparing the refreshments while children are doing other party activities.

15. Read some of the Knowledge Facts to the children if there is any wait time.

HEART GAMES

THE HEART BEAT, FLUTTER, PUMP, THUMP GAME (K-6)

SUPPLIES
No materials required

**Here's some slam-bang entertainment for all kids.
Have them stand in a circle and teach them the following:**

DIRECTIONS

1. Touch your heart two times and repeat the words "heart, heart."
2. Tap on your head two times and repeat the words "beat, beat."
3. Wave your arms into the air (like a bird flying) and repeat the words "flutter, flutter."
4. Flex your arm muscles two times while repeating the words "pump, pump."
5. Stomp your feet two times and repeat the words "thump, thump."
6. Repeat Steps 1 through 5. Go faster as you get the hang of it.
7. Play for 5 minutes or eliminate players who miss an action or words.

Note: The eliminated players can help spot others who make mistakes.

Look at the size of your fist, it is the size of your heart. Your fist and your heart grow at the same rate.

SURPRISE HEARTS (K-6)

SUPPLIES
Plain white paper
Two different colored crayons per child

DIRECTIONS

1. Give each child a piece of paper and two crayons.
2. Have the children close their eyes and use one crayon to draw a heart on the piece of paper.
3. With their eyes still closed, they color in the heart with the other crayon. Of course, the goal is to stay within the heart's lines.
4. Last, but most important, have them sign their artwork with their eyes still closed.

HEART GAMES

QUESTIONABLE HEARTS (3-6)

SUPPLIES

Copy of questions and answers

Pens or pencils (one per child)

DIRECTIONS

1. Give each child a copy of the questions and answers from below.
2. Their job is to match the correct answer to its question by connecting a line to each.
3. Before beginning, give them an example such as "What is a sweetheart?" Answer: Heartbeat.

What heart has a burning in the stomach or is on fire?	Heart attack
What heart is sincere?	Heartless
What heart has contractions?	Heartland
What heart has insects that live in a dog?	Heartburn
What heart is a central land area?	Heartwood
What heart is cruel?	Heartbeat
What heart is the wood of a trunk?	Heart worm
What heart has emotional distress and hurts?	Heartfelt
What heart makes sound or whispers?	Heartache
What heart suddenly stops working?	Heart murmur

MEND A BROKEN HEART (1-6)

SUPPLIES

Scissors

Assorted cotton fabrics

Safety pins (one per child)

Needles and thread

DIRECTIONS

1. Pre-cut heart shapes out of the assorted fabrics (one per child).
2. Zigzag cut each heart in half and pin it together.
3. Give each child a heart along with a needle and thread to mend their hearts.

Note: Pre-thread the needle and knot the thread for younger age children.

MY BUBBLY HEART (K-6)

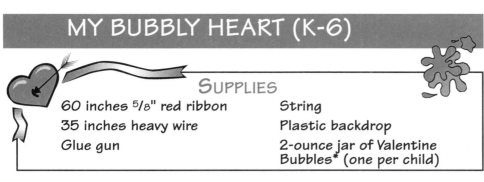

SUPPLIES

60 inches ⅝" red ribbon

35 inches heavy wire

Glue gun

String

Plastic backdrop

2-ounce jar of Valentine Bubbles* (one per child)

DIRECTIONS

1. Wind the red ribbon around the heavy wire and secure with glue. Shape into a heart.

2. Attach the string to the top of the heart and hang from a high place such as the ceiling rafters. Hang it low enough to be face level with the children. Spread the plastic backdrop underneath the heart.

3. Each child gets a jar of bubbles and takes a turn blowing bubbles through the heart. Points can be given for each bubble that successfully makes it through the heart.

Any bubbles can be used, but Oriental Trading® Company, Inc. sells miniature Valentine Bubbles (they're cute!). For availability and pricing call 1-800-228-2269, or write them at P.O. Box 3407, Omaha, Nebraska 68103-3407.

HEART RELAY (K-6)

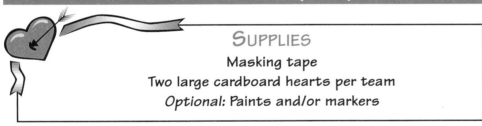

SUPPLIES

Masking tape

Two large cardboard hearts per team

Optional: Paints and/or markers

DIRECTIONS

1. Divide the children into teams.

2. Determine your starting and ending lines and mark them with masking tape. Try to utilize the whole length of the classroom.

3. Give the first child on each team two cardboard hearts. On "Go," he places one of the hearts on the floor in front of him and hops on it, either with one foot or two – he decides. He then places the other heart in front of the one he is on and hops on the second one. He continues to do this to the ending line and then back to the finish line.

4. The next player is given the hearts and proceeds to do the same. The first team to finish wins.

Optional: Decorate the hearts with paints and/or markers.

29

SUPPLIES FOR HEART GAMES

THE HEART BEAT, FLUTTER, PUMP GAME (K-6)

No materials required

SURPRISE HEARTS (K-6)

Plain white paper
Two different colored crayons per child

QUESTIONABLE HEARTS (3-6)

Copy of questions and answers
Pens or pencils (one per child)

MEND A BROKEN HEART (1-6)

Scissors
Assorted cotton fabrics
Safety pins (one per child)
Needles and thread

MY BUBBLY HEART (1-6)

60 inches $5/8$" red ribbon
35 inches heavy wire
Glue gun
String
Plastic backdrop
2-ounce jar of Valentine Bubbles
(one per child)

HEART RELAY (K-6)

Masking tape
Two large cardboard hearts per team
Optional: Paints and/or markers

Don't forget the camera and film.

CUPID GAMES

CUPID BOW & ARROW (1-6)

SUPPLIES

Scissors (or knife)

Oversized cardboard box

Black permanent marker

Masking tape

Toy bow and arrow set

Optional: Paints, markers, cut-out hearts and/or stickers.

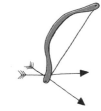

DIRECTIONS

1. Cut heart shapes out of the oversized cardboard box. Add point values by each heart opening.

2. Position the box about 10 to 15 feet away from the children. Using masking tape, make a line on the floor.

3. Have each child take a turn shooting arrows through the heart openings. Some children may need help using the bow and arrow.

4. Have a parent or child retrieve the arrows and bring them back to the starting line.

Optional: Decorate the box with paints, markers, cut-out hearts and/or stickers.

Variation: Older grades may want to keep score.

CUPID'S QUEST (K-6)

SUPPLIES

Permanent markers

Five 3-inch paper hearts (per child)

DIRECTIONS

1. Write out the word "Cupid," one letter per heart, one set of five hearts per child.

2. Mix up the hearts and hide them throughout the room. Do this before the party so the children will not know where to search.

3. On "Go," have the children search for the hearts. The object is for each child to find a complete set of the letters to spell the word "Cupid." A child may swap with other players, but must end up with only five hearts.

4. Play for 5 minutes or until all the children have the word "Cupid."

Note: For younger kids, use brighter paper to help them locate the heart letters, and write the word "Cupid" on the board.

CUPID GAMES

LICORICE CUPID CONTEST (K-6)

SUPPLIES

Scissors

5 x 7-inch white poster board

Paper hole puncher

Long red lace licorice (one strand per couple)

DIRECTIONS

1. Cut Cupids out of the white poster board using the pattern on page 34. You need one per couple.

2. Punch a hole at the top of each Cupid's head.

3. Slide a strand of licorice through the hole so the Cupid is in the center of the strand.

4. Have the children find a partner. Give each couple a Licorice Cupid.

5. On "Go," the players each place one end of the licorice into their mouths with their hands behind their backs. Then they chew the licorice, working their way to the Cupid.

6. Have the camera ready!

Caution: This is not meant to be a race. The children will have mouthfuls of licorice, and you want no one to choke. Explain this to the class beforehand.

CUPID'S CASTLE (K-6)

SUPPLIES

Pencil

5 x 7-inch white poster board (per group)

Scissors

Lots of empty toilet paper rolls and paper towel rolls

Clear packing tape

Optional: Red spray paint

DIRECTIONS

1. Trace a Cupid onto the white poster board using the pattern on page 34, then cut out. You will need one per group.

2. Divide the class into small groups.

3. Give each group toilet paper rolls, paper towel rolls, and a Cupid. Have them create and build a castle to slide Cupid into. They may use tape to hold the castle together.

Optional: Spray paint the rolls red, and let dry.

MUSICAL CUPIDS (K-6)

SUPPLIES

Scissors   Red poster board

White poster board   Music

DIRECTIONS

1. Pre-cut Cupids from the white poster board (one per boy). Pre-cut Hearts from the red poster board (one per girl). Make them large enough for the children to stand on.

2. Lay the cut-outs on the floor in a circle, alternating Cupids and Hearts.

3. Have the boys stand on the Cupids and the girls on the Hearts.

4. Before you begin playing, you need to take one Cupid and one Heart away. You have now taken a total of two away.

5. Have the children walk around the circle while you play the music.

6. When you stop the music, each child tries to stand on a cut-out. Boys must find a Cupid to stand on and girls must find a Heart.

7. The boy who doesn't find a Cupid and the girl who doesn't find a Heart are eliminated from the game.

8. Take away one more Cupid and one more Heart and play another round. There always needs to be one less Cupid than boys, and one less Heart than girls remaining in the game.

9. Continue playing until there is one Cupid (boy) and one Heart (girl) left.

Note: The boys and girls who are eliminated can take turns collecting the Cupids and Hearts.

Variation: If there is an odd number of boys and girls, divide the children into two groups. The boys (Cupids) will play against the boys and the girls (Hearts) will play against the girls. Continue playing Musical Cupids until you have one winner in each group.

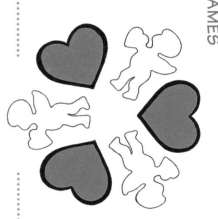

WHERE'S CUPID? (K-1)

SUPPLIES

Pencil   Scissors

5 x 7-inch white poster   Masking tape
board (per group)

DIRECTIONS

1. Trace a Cupid onto the white poster board using the pattern on page 34, then cut out.

2. Have all the children turn around and close their eyes.

3. Hide Cupid by taping him onto the teacher's back.

4. Have the teacher sit at her desk. Tell the children to open their eyes, turn around, and go find Cupid.

Note: This can be a fast game.

33

CUPID GAMES

CUPID PATTERN

SUPPLIES FOR CUPID GAMES

CUPID BOW & ARROW (1-6)

Scissors (or knife)

Oversized cardboard box

Black permanent marker

Masking tape

Toy bow and arrow set

Optional: Paints, markers, cut-out hearts and/or stickers.

CUPID'S QUEST (K-6)

Permanent markers

Five 3-inch paper hearts (per child)

LICORICE CUPID CONTEST (K-6)

Scissors

5 x 7-inch white poster board

Paper hole puncher

Long red lace licorice
(one strand per couple)

CUPID'S CASTLE (K-6)

Pencil

5 x 7-inch white poster board
(per group)

Scissors

Lots of empty toilet paper rolls
and paper towel rolls

Clear packing tape

Optional: Red spray paint

MUSICAL CUPIDS (K-6)

Scissors

White poster board

Red poster board

Music

WHERE'S CUPID? (K-1)

Pencil

5 x 7-inch white poster board

Scissors

Masking tape

Don't forget the camera and film.

International Friendship Week is the last week of February.

LOVE & FRIENDSHIP GAMES

WHERE'S YOUR PARTNER? (1-6)

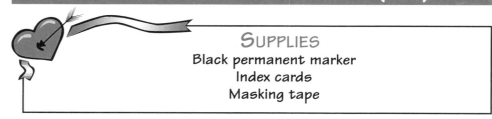

SUPPLIES
Black permanent marker
Index cards
Masking tape

DIRECTIONS

1. Write out names on index cards, one name per card, using the list of pairs below (or others of your choice).

2. Have the children sit in a circle, then tape one card onto each child's back. Do not allow them to see each other's cards until you say "Go."

3. Give the kids approximately 10 minutes to find their match. They do this by asking "yes" or "no" questions of the other classmates. Some example questions might include: "Am I famous?" "Am I dead?"

Note: Be careful placing names on children that might embarrass them. It is also best to place a girl's name on a girl, and a boy's name on a boy.

Mickey-Minnie	King of Hearts-Queen of Hearts
Cinderella-Prince Charming	Raggedy Ann-Andy
Jack-Jill	Popeye-Olive Oil
Romeo-Juliet	Barbie -Ken
Sonny-Cher	Donny-Marie
Batman-Robin	Princess Leia-Luke Skywalker
Homer-Marge	Beauty-Beast
Rudy-Buzz	Bert-Ernie
Kermit-Miss Piggy	ChewBacca-Hansolo
Winnie the Pooh-Tigger	Piglet-Eiore
Big Bad Wolf-Three Pigs	Lucy-Ethel
Tarzan-Jane	Adam-Eve
Anthony-Cleopatra	Mork-Mindy

Fred-Wilma-Pebbles (for odd number of children)

BOYS' & GIRLS' FORTUNES (2-6)

SUPPLIES
Class List*

Pen or pencil (one per child)

Lined paper

Tape

DIRECTIONS

1. Prior to the party, get a class list* and write each child's first name on the top line of a piece of paper. Fold the paper over twice to cover the name, and tape lightly. If the child is a boy, write "girl" on the front of the fold. If a girl, write "boy."

2. Skip about 10 to 15 lines and write the following on the left side of the paper, using one entry per line:

   Boy's first name or Girl's first name
   Any date (past or future)
   Any number
   Another number
   Favorite color
   Worst color
   An occupation
   Another occupation
   State or country
   Any activity

3. Have the kids sit in a circle. Randomly pass out the papers and pens, one per child. It won't matter whose name is on the fold. A boy can get a girl's name and a girl can get a boy's name.

4. Ask the children to fill in the first line. They may use the floor for a writing surface. They will then pass their papers to the right.

5. The children fill out the next category, then once again, pass their papers to the right. Follow this procedure until all the lines have been filled out.

6. Collect the papers from all the children, untape the tops, and read each fortune.

7. Listen for giggles.

*If you can't tell the gender from the name, call the teacher to clarify in order to save any embarrassment.

Tip: You may wish to write yourself a "script" on a narrow piece of paper, to cover the list on the previous page as you read the paper. Use the following list, one item per line: "name under fold" married _____; on; they have _____ daughters; and _____ sons; all with _____ eyes; and _____ hair; "name under fold" is an _____; and "name on top line" is a _____; they live in _____; the entire family enjoys _____. (Fill in the blank lines with the children's answers.)

Example: Susie married Ronny on Wednesday, December 12, 1602. They have 580 daughters and 12 sons, all with red eyes and yellow hair. Susie is an actress and Ronny is a doctor. They live in Kentucky. The entire family enjoys swimming.

LOVE & FRIENDSHIP GAMES

THE LOVE BOAT CRUISE (K-6)

SUPPLIES

Play cruise director's hat

Play captain's hat

Cruise news
(see example)

Tickets
(see example)

Ports of call itinerary
(see example)

Hawaiian lei

Food for midnight buffet

Cards/poker chips

Suitcase

Beach chair

Play money

Life jacket

Hula hoop

Limbo stick

Snorkel equipment

Beach towel

Fan (for breeze)

Bingo cards

Bottle of non-alcoholic wine

Fitness clothes

Golf clubs

Stuffed animals (fish, dolphins, lizards, whales, birds, etc.)

Trophies

Camera

DIRECTIONS

1. Choose some or all of the above supplies, or use some of your own ideas.

2. Make a copy of the cruise news, ports of call itinerary, and tickets, or use some from home if available.

3. Divide the class into groups. One at a time, give each group the cruise supplies and approximately five minutes to create a skit.

4. Have each group perform for the other groups. Vote on the best Love Boat Cruise skit, winners get trophies.

Note: While one group is creating a skit, keep other groups busy with Valentine Word Search on page 66.

BON VOYAGE!

Ports of call • 7 Night Dream Vacation • Love Boat (6/18)			
Day	Ports of Call	Arrive	Depart
Sat	Los Angeles, CA		3:30 p.m.
Sun	At sea		
Mon	At sea		
Tues	Puerto Vallarta, Mexico	7:00 a.m.	6:00 p.m.
Wed	Mazatlan, Mexico	7:00 a.m.	5:00 p.m.
Thurs	Cabo San Lucas, Mexico	8:00 a.m.	3:00 p.m.
Fri	At sea		
Sat	Los Angeles, CA	9:00 a.m.	

LOVE BOAT CRUISE

Departing from Los Angeles, CA on June 18 for 7 days.

You will have the late dinner seating.

Please be at the boat by 2:00 p.m. Boat departs at 3:30 p.m.

Please be sure to bring your smiles!

YOU MUST HAVE THIS TICKET TO BOARD THE BOAT.

CRUISE NEWS

for Sunday 6/19 • Welcome to a Dream Vacation!

Activity	Time	Location
Breakfast	6:30 a.m. - 10:30 a.m.	
Lunch	11:00 a.m. - 2:00 p.m.	Rainbow Deck
Dinner	Main seating - 5:30 p.m.	Twinkle Deck
	Late seating - 7:30 p.m.	Dining Room
		Dining Room

*Meet the Captain at the beginning of both dinners, get your pictures taken for $15.00

Activity	Time	Location
Desserts Forever	2:00 p.m. - 5:00 p.m.	
Midnight Buffet	12:00 (midnight)	Heavenly Deck
Early Breakfast Buffet	2:00 a.m. - 3:00 a.m.	Dining Room
Life Boat/Jacket Drill (All Passengers)	TBA	Rock n' Roll Deck
		TBA
Bingo	2:30 p.m. and 5:30 p.m. $1,000.00 Jackpots!	Bingo Hall
Meet the Staff Party	12:00 noon Free Kitty Cocktails and Potato Chips	Rainbow Deck
Snorkeling	9:00 a.m. - 3:00 p.m. Rent your equipment early	Sunshine Deck
Pool Opens	9:00 a.m. - 10:00 p.m.	Sunshine Deck
Slide Opens	11:00 a.m. - 2:00 p.m., 4:00 p.m. Check out towels at pool	Sunshine Deck
Casino/Card Room	*Opens 2 hours after leaving California, until 2 hours before arriving back at California	Make Me Rich Deck
Limbo Contest	3:00 p.m.	Rock n' Roll Deck
Hula-Hoop Contest	3:30 p.m.	Rock n' Roll Deck
Lip Synch Contest	4:00 p.m.	Rock n' Roll Deck

*All contests are for both children and adults. Trophies will be awarded!

Activity	Time	Location
Exercise Room	6:00 a.m. - 11:00 p.m.	Get Fit Deck
Cruise Director explains about Ports of Call	2:00 p.m.	Twinkle Deck
Dolphin/Whale Watch	6:30 p.m.	Heavenly Deck
Movie	1:00 p.m.	

*Featuring "The Friendship Bunch"
Popcorn $1.00 • Pop $.50

VALENTINE MATCH GAME (K-6)

LOVE & FRIENDSHIP GAMES

Laughing and giggling,
The kids all came
To the party, to play
The Valentine Match game.

Karen Timm

SUPPLIES

Two pictures of a heart ... Two heart cut-outs

Two bags of flour ... Two roses

Two pieces of Hugs®candy ... Two pictures of two people hugging

Two pictures of a ring ... Two toy rings

Two Hershey's Kisses® ... Two pictures of a couple kissing

Two chocolate candies (sweet) ... Two bags of sugar

Two pictures of Cupid ... Two cut-out Cupids

Two Valentines (folded accordion style) ... Two electric fans with
                                    Valentine stickers

Two desks

Divider*

DIRECTIONS

1. Set up the divider.

2. Place the above objects on separate desks, one set on each side. For example, one bag of flour on one desk and the other bag on the other desk.

3. Form teams of two.

4. Position one player from a team on one side of the divider, and another player from the other team on the other side.

5. Tell the rest of the class not to "help" the team playing, because it will hurt their chances of winning.

6. Read the following list of items one at a time. Have each player select the item he feels fits the description best and hold it up. If both players hold up the same item, they score a point. (When all the teams have played, the one with the most points wins.)

Example: "Heart" – If both members select the cut-out heart they get a point; if one selects the cut-out heart, and the other selects the picture of the heart, then no points are scored.

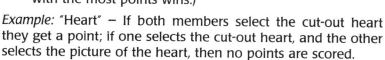

Heart

Flower

Hugs

Ring

Kiss

Something Sweet

Cupid

Valentine Fan

*A divider could be a dark sheet or blanket (not see-through) attached from the ceiling to the floor, or some heavy poster boards or pieces of cardboard attached together. The divider must be tall enough and wide enough to block the children's view from either side. Place the divider so the rest of the class can see the action on both sides.

LIPS (K-6)

SUPPLIES

Permanent markers

3 x 4-foot white poster board

Masking tape

Chocolate-covered lips (one per child)

DIRECTIONS

1. Draw a picture of a woman onto the poster board, leaving her with no mouth. Color her with markers.

2. Lay the picture on the ground, then using masking tape, make a starting line on the floor about three feet from the woman's picture.

3. Have the children line up at the line. Give each child one chocolate-covered lips and have him take a turn tossing the lips at the woman. The object is to get the lips to where the woman's lips should be.

4. Move the woman closer to the line if the children are having a difficult time.

PINKY-LINKY (K-6)

SUPPLIES

Balloons

DIRECTIONS

1. Have everyone choose a partner and then have the couples sit on the floor, back to back, with a balloon placed between them.

2. Have the couples reach their hands behind their backs and link their pinkies.

3. Pushing against each other's backs and walking their feet in, they try to stand up without breaking the balloon.

Variation: Have the partners stand with the balloon between their backs, lower to the ground, and then return to the standing position without breaking the balloon.

Note: Blow up the balloons ahead of time.

SUPPLIES FOR LOVE & FRIENDSHIP GAMES

WHERE'S YOUR PARTNER? (1-6)
- Black permanent marker
- Index cards
- Masking tape

BOYS' & GIRLS' FORTUNES (2-6)
- Class list
- Pen or pencil (one per child)
- Lined paper
- Tape

THE LOVE BOAT CRUISE (K-6)
- Play cruise director's hat
- Play captain's hat
- Cruise news (see example)
- Tickets (see example)
- Ports of call itinerary (see example)
- Hawaiian lei
- Food for midnight buffet
- Cards/poker chips
- Suitcase
- Beach chair
- Play money
- Life jacket
- Hula hoop
- Limbo stick
- Snorkel equipment
- Beach towel
- Fan (for breeze)
- Bingo cards
- Bottle of non-alcoholic wine
- Fitness clothes
- Golf clubs
- Stuffed animals (fish, dolphins, lizards, whales, birds, etc.)
- Trophies
- Camera

VALENTINE MATCH GAME (K-6)
- Two pictures of a heart
- Two heart cut-outs
- Two bags of flour
- Two roses
- Two pieces of Hugs® candy
- Two pictures of two people hugging
- Two pictures of a ring
- Two toy rings
- Two Hershey's Kisses® candies
- Two wax lips
- Two pictures of a couple kissing
- Two chocolate candies(sweet)
- Two bags of sugar
- Two pictures of Cupid
- Two cut-out cupids
- Two Valentines (folded accordion style)
- Two electric fans with Valentine stickers
- Two desks
- Divider

LIPS (K-6)
- Permanent markers
- 3 x 4-foot white poster board
- Masking tape
- Chocolate-covered lips (one per child)

PINKY-LINKY (K-6)
- Balloons

ANIMAL GAMES

GROUNDHOG NEEDS A HEART (K-3)

SUPPLIES

Large heart stickers

Large stuffed groundhog (or Teddy Bear)

Desk

Masking tape

Blindfold

Optional: Flashlight

DIRECTIONS

1. Give each player a heart sticker.
2. Place the groundhog on a desk.
3. Mark your starting line with masking tape (adjust according to age).
4. Blindfold the first player, and spin him around three times. Direct the player towards the groundhog and instruct him to place the heart on the area where the groundhog's heart should be.

Note: Secure the groundhog down if needed. You can tape the legs to the desk or have a parent hold the groundhog. Be careful if another child holds the stuffed animal − he may move it around to help the player locate the heart area.

Optional: Kindergartners may enjoy taking turns shining a flashlight (the sun) on the groundhog while another classmate is about to give the groundhog a heart.

FLIPPER (K-6)

SUPPLIES

Masking tape

Four buckets, two half-filled with water

Two pair of flippers

Two 8-ounce paper cups

DIRECTIONS

1. Divide the children into two teams.
2. Mark off a starting line for each team with the masking tape. Put an empty bucket, a pair of flippers, and a paper cup at each starting line.
3. Mark two additional lines approximately 10 feet away. Place the buckets with water at these lines.
4. Have the children remove their shoes.
5. On the word "Go," the first player in each team puts on the flippers. Each player will pick up the cup, waddle down to the bucket of water, scoop water into the cup, waddle back, pour the water into the empty bucket, and place the cup on the floor. He then takes the flippers off for the next player, and goes to the end of the line.
6. The next player repeats the process.
7. After an allotted time, whichever team has the most water in their bucket, wins.

ANIMAL GAMES

SLIPPERY SNAKES (K-6)

SUPPLIES

Two thin long balloons
(one per team)

Greasy hand lotion

Paper towels

DIRECTIONS

1. Blow up the balloons before the party begins.
2. Rub the balloons with hand lotion.
3. Divide the class into two teams and have them stand in a straight line facing forward. Give the children hand lotion to put on their hands but tell them not to rub it in completely.
4. Give the last player of each team a slippery snake balloon. That player passes it over the player's head in front of him. The second player takes the balloon and must pass it forward to the third player through that player's legs. The players alternate over their heads and under their legs until the balloon gets to the first team member. The first team to finish wins.
5. If a balloon slips out of a player's hands, the team has to start over.
6. When the game is complete, everyone gets a paper towel to wipe the lotion off their hands.

Tip: Have extra balloons in case of breakage.

What does Valentine's Day mean to you?

"Loving."
  Samantha McCarthy, Age 9½

"Hearts, red, flowers, and cards."
  Andrew Schildkret, Age 6

GOOSE ON THE LOOSE (K-3)

SUPPLIES

Pencil

White poster board

Scissors

Red permanent marker

Optional: Tape

DIRECTIONS

1. Before the party, trace the goose onto the white poster board and cut out (one goose per child).
2. Using the marker, color the heart hanging from each goose's neck.
3. Cut each goose into five separate pieces, making each "puzzle" as identical as possible to the others.
4. When it is time for the party, tell the kids the "goose is on the loose" and toss the goose pieces into the air.
5. Each child needs to find five pieces of a goose, and put the "puzzle" together. (The pieces don't need to be from the same goose, just the five "parts" of a goose.)

Optional: Children can tape the puzzle together to take their goose home.

SUPPLIES FOR ANIMAL GAMES

GROUNDHOG NEEDS A HEART (K-3)

- Large heart stickers
- Large stuffed groundhog (or Teddy Bear)
- Desk
- Masking tape
- Blindfold
- *Optional: Flashlight*

FLIPPER (K-6)

- Masking tape
- Four buckets, two half-filled with water
- Two pair of flippers
- Two 8-ounce paper cups

SLIPPERY SNAKES (K-6)

- Two thin long balloons (one per team)
- Greasy hand lotion
- Paper towels

GOOSE ON THE LOOSE (K-3)

- Pencil
- White poster board
- Scissors
- Red permanent marker
- *Optional: Tape*

ANIMAL MOTIONS AND HEART RACE (K-4)

- Scissors
- Assorted colors of construction paper
- Black permanent marker

VALENTINE ANIMAL CUT-OUTS (K-6)

- Scissors
- Assorted colors of construction paper
- School glue

Don't forget the camera and film.

POST OFFICE GAMES

*Send me a Valentine
Right from your heart –
Say you're my friend,
That we'll never be apart.*

Karen Timm

AIR MAIL YOUR VALENTINE (K-6)

SUPPLIES

Pencil	Red spray paint
9 x 3-inch piece of foam board	Large canister
Scissors or x-acto® knife	Assorted colors of construction paper
Two empty toilet paper rolls	Tape
Three empty paper towel rolls	Masking tape
Glue gun	Optional: Old map
Paper towel	

DIRECTIONS

1. Trace pattern piece #1 (arrow) onto the foam board and cut out. You will need three.
2. Trace pattern piece #2 (wing) onto the toilet paper rolls and cut out. You will need six.
3. Cut four slits into one end of each paper towel roll, equal distances apart and approximately 1½ inches deep. Set aside.
4. Cut a ¾-inch slit at point "a" in three of the wings.
5. Cut a ¾-inch slit at point "b" in the three other wings.
6. Insert point "a" of a wing into point "b" of another wing. Repeat with the remaining wings. You will have three sets of tail wings.
7. Slide a tail wing into each paper towel tube, one wing per slit. Glue to hold.
8. Wrap the base of the arrow point with a paper towel and slide it into the opposite end of the roll from the wings. Glue to hold.
9. Spray paint the arrows and let dry.
10. Decorate the canister with construction paper to look like the world.
11. Mark a starting line on the floor about 5 feet from the canister, using masking tape.
12. To play the game, give the children, one at a time, the three arrows to airmail their Valentine (flying them into the can).

Optional: Wrap an old map (or parts of it) around the canister

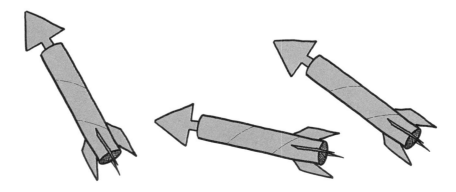

What Do I Do?™

#1

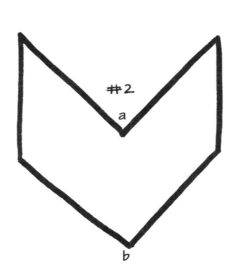

#2

a

b

49

POST OFFICE (K-4)

SUPPLIES

Large empty refrigerator box (found at any appliance store)

2-3 cans red spray paint

Knife

White paper

Red permanent marker

Tape

Assorted acrylic paints

American flag

Play money (one bill, any amount, per student)

Rectangle Valentine stickers resembling postage stamps*

At least three small baskets

Optional: Small chair

* Enough for each child to "mail" Valentines to all the other children. For example, if there are 30 students, you will need 30 stickers x 30 students = 900 stickers.

DIRECTIONS

1. Design the refrigerator box to look like a post office by spray painting the entire box red. Let it dry and apply another coat if needed.

2. Make a back entrance so a parent can step into the box and kneel or sit on the chair.

3. Cut a large rectangular opening near the top of the front of the box for the parent to play Postmaster.

4. Cut a slot in the front of the box for a mail drop.

5. Make signs that say "Post Office" and "Mail Slot" using the white paper and red marker. Tape to the Post Office.

6. Paint assorted hearts on the box.

7. Secure the flag to the top of the box with tape.

You can play Post Office several ways. Here is one:

1. Each child receives one money bill.

2. Have a parent play Postmaster and have the children buy stamps (stickers) with their money.

3. Have the children put their stamps on their Valentine card envelopes and deposit them in the mail slot. Tell parents to help the slower children to keep this task flowing well.

4. When a child distributes cards into the slot the Postmaster catches them in a basket. The Postmaster then hands the basket to a parent helper, who distributes the cards to the children's bags or boxes. The Postmaster then grabs another basket for the next child's mail and so on.

5. If possible, have a real mailman come visit and talk to the class and deliver their mail. Kindergarten classes are thrilled.

Note: The above is played with no names on the cards. If the children will be writing names on the outside of their envelopes, names must be on the children's bags or boxes for distribution. You will need several parents to help distribute. Also, line up the boxes/bags with children's names in alphabetical order. This is very *important* in order to ensure smooth and quick delivery.

Tip: Play Post Office at the beginning of the party so the Postmaster's helpers can be distributing the Valentine cards "calmly" while the party is continuing.

Since 1973, the U.S. Postal Service has offered a Popular Love Stamp Series. If you would like to express love in a stamp design, Get out your art supplies and start creating. Send your art to:

Editor
Kids' Poet
P.O. Box 2108
Vienna, VA 22183-2108

POST OFFICE (continued)

Here is another way to play Post Office:

1. You may choose to have the Post Office set up for a whole week before the party and let the kids deposit their Valentines without buying stamps (stickers). The cards should be dumping into a large container inside the Post Office to be sorted later. You wouldn't need the baskets for this method of play. *Important:* Names must be on the Valentine card envelopes if being deposited this way. If there are no names on the cards you will have a mess.

2. You may also choose to have the Postmaster come into the classroom and open the Post Office at certain times to allow kids to buy stamps (stickers) from him and receive a postmark on each mailed piece. You would need an ink stamp, preferably with a Valentine theme, for this method of playing Post Office.

Conversaton hearts, orginated in the latter part of the 1860's, the sayings were first composed on paper and were tucked into candy shells. By 1902, a method was devised to print the messages on candy hearts. Over eight billion conversation hearts are produced each year. Wow!

CANDY HEART SENTENCES (K-6)

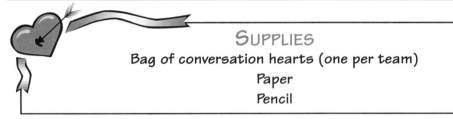

SUPPLIES
Bag of conversation hearts (one per team)

Paper

Pencil

DIRECTIONS

1. Each team is given a bag of conversation hearts.

2. Give the teams an allotted amount of time (3-5 min) to make as many complete sentences or sayings as possible. Once the hearts have been used in a sentence or saying, they cannot be used again.

3. Score each team either by the amount of hearts used or the amount of words used in all the sentences and sayings.

Note: Younger children may need help with their sentences.

As of 1998, the candy company NECCO has approximately 125 different sayings it prints on its conversation hearts. NECCO was founded in 1847, over 150 years ago!

MAIL THE VALENTINE LETTERS (K-3)

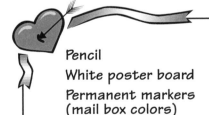

SUPPLIES
Pencil

White poster board

Permanent markers (mail box colors)

Small envelopes (one per child)

Double-stick tape

Blindfold (mailbox colors)

DIRECTIONS

1. Draw a mailbox on the white poster board and color it with markers.

2. Have the children write their own names on the outside of their envelopes and hold onto them. Put double-stick tape on the back of the envelopes.

3. Blindfold a child, spin him around, give him his envelope, and then lead him to the mailbox. Repeat for each child. The player then sticks the envelope on the box, pretending to mail it. The child whose letter is closest to the slot wins.

51

VALENTINE BALLOON RACE (K-6)

SUPPLIES

Red permanent marker

Nine ½ x ½-inch pieces of paper (per team)

Balloon (one per team)

School glue

Standard size envelope (one per team)

Heart sticker (one per team)

DIRECTIONS

1. Write out the word "Valentine" on the nine pieces of paper, one letter per square.

2. Push all nine pieces into a balloon.

3. Blow up the balloon and knot the end. Repeat for each team.

4. The teams are to pop the balloon, collect their letters, and glue them on the envelope to spell the word "Valentine." They also need to place the heart sticker on the stamp corner of the envelope. The first team to finish wins.

Note: Prepare steps 1 to 3 ahead of time.

Caution: When blowing up the balloons, be careful you don't inhale the papers.

Drop the pretty handkerchief,
The frilly one with lace.
Make another Valentine, and
Play Valentine Balloon Race.

Karen Timm

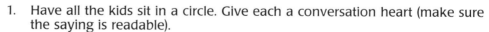

HEART REPEATS (1-6)

SUPPLIES
Bag of conversation hearts

DIRECTIONS

1. Have all the kids sit in a circle. Give each a conversation heart (make sure the saying is readable).

2. Any child can start. He reads the saying on his heart aloud. The next child in the circle repeats that saying and reads the saying on his heart. The third child repeats the first and second sayings, and then reads his own. Keep going around the circle with each child repeating the previous sayings, in order, in addition to his own.

3. If a child makes a mistake, he is eliminated from the game along with his saying. Have him stay seated in the circle, but slightly back from the group. He can help spot mistakes.

SUPPLIES FOR POST OFFICE GAMES

AIR MAIL YOUR VALENTINE (K-6)

- 9 x 3-inch piece of foam board
- Scissors or x-acto® knife
- Pencil
- Three empty paper towel rolls
- Two empty toilet paper rolls
- Glue gun
- Paper towel
- Large canister
- Assorted colors of construction paper
- Tape
- Red spray paint
- Masking tape
- *Optional: Old map*

POST OFFICE (K-4)

- Large empty refrigerator box (found at any appliance store)
- 2-3 cans red spray paint
- Knife
- White paper
- Red permanent marker
- Tape
- Assorted acrylic paints
- American flag
- Play money (one bill, any amount, per student)
- Rectangle Valentine stickers resembling postage stamps
- At least three small baskets
- *Optional: Small chair*

CANDY HEART SENTENCES (K-6)

- Bag of conversation hearts (one per team)
- Paper
- Pencil

MAIL THE VALENTINE LETTERS (K-3)

- Pencil
- White poster board
- Permanent markers (mail box colors)
- Small envelopes (one per child)
- Double-stick tape
- Blindfold (mailbox colors)

VALENTINE BALLOON RACE (K-6)

- Red permanent marker
- Nine ½ x ½-inch pieces of paper (per team)
- Balloon (one per team)
- School glue
- Standard size envelope (one per team)
- Heart sticker (one per team)

HEART REPEATS (1-6)

- Bag of conversation hearts

FEBRUARY & PRESIDENTS' GAMES

CALENDAR TOSS (K-6)

SUPPLIES

22 x 28-inch white poster board

Black permanent marker

Red permanent marker

Three 2-inch wooden hearts (found at craft stores)

Masking tape

DIRECTIONS

1. Recreate the calendar month of February onto the poster board, leaving the square for the 14th empty. Use the black permanent marker for the lines, numbers, and month.

2. Draw a large heart with the red permanent marker in the 14th square, filling in this heart. Draw and fill in smaller hearts in the blank squares.

3. Color all sides of the wooden hearts using the red permanent marker.

4. Place the calendar flat on the floor and mark a starting line with the masking tape.

5. Each child gets to toss all three hearts onto the calendar. They choose whether to throw them together or separately. Add up the numbers the hearts land on for the child's score. If a heart lands on the 14th, give 14 points plus an extra 100 points for Valentine's Day. The child with the most points wins.

*February's the month
But fourteen's the day.
Let's have a great party,
Get ready to play!*

Karen Timm

What does Valentine's Day mean to you?

"A date, like a calendar."

Priscilla Ripple, Age 7

LINCOLN'S HAT PENNY DROP (K-6)

SUPPLIES

Two 9 x 12-inch sheets black construction paper

Tape

Empty oatmeal container

Knife

Pennies (six per child)

DIRECTIONS

1. Wrap and tape black construction paper around the empty oatmeal container.

2. Also, wrap paper around the lid, taping on the bottom.

3. Cut a small heart shape into the lid large enough for pennies to drop through.

4. Cut a circle shape out of construction paper to lay on top of the container for the hat's brim. Cut a slit through this paper to match up with the lid's heart shape. Tape it in place at the slit and underneath onto the lid (so you can open the container).

5. To play the game, give each player six pennies and have them, one at a time, stand directly over Lincoln's Hat. The player must stand straight, no bending.

6. The player then drops the pennies, one by one, trying to get them through the slot.

Variation: This game can be a team race. Make two hats and have teams play against each other. The team with the most pennies in its hat wins.

President Abraham Lincoln was photographed 39 times without his beard and 80 times with a beard. He is seen seated in 94 pictures, standing 24 times, and once lying down, after his death.

FEBRUARY & PRESIDENTS' GAMES

HUMAN VALENTINE TIC-TAC-TOE (1-6)

SUPPLIES

Red permanent marker

6 x 6-inch square plain white paper (one per child)

Masking tape
(or chalk if played outside)

DIRECTIONS

1. Alternately mark "X's" and "O's" on the squares of paper until there is one piece per child. Make the letters large and bold.

2. To play this game inside, make a large Tic-Tac-Toe grid on the floor using masking tape. To play this game outside, make a large Tic-Tac-Toe grid on the sidewalk using chalk.

3. Line the class up and tape an "X" on the front of the first child, an "O" on the second child, and so on.

4. Have the first player stand in one of the nine spaces. The next player, with the opposite mark, chooses another space. Then the third player, and so forth, until either the "X's" or "O's" have three marks in a row (horizontal, vertical, or diagonal) or the grid is filled in completely. Those players now move to the end of the line and a new game starts.

5. Play for an allotted amount of time. Keep track of how many times the "X's" and/or "O's" win. Winners can be given prizes or be the first to line up for refreshments.

55

VALENTINE CANDY RELAY (K-6)

SUPPLIES

Masking tape

Two spoons

Two bowls

Two bags of small Valentine candy

Two 2-cup measuring cups

DIRECTIONS

1. Designate a starting line with masking tape.

2. Divide the class into two teams and stand them behind the starting line.

3. Each team is given a spoon and stands next to a bowl of one bag of candy.

4. Place the two measuring cups across the room from the teams.

5. On "Go," the first player of each team scoops out candy from the bowl with the spoon, walks as quickly as possible across the room, and pours the candy into his team's measuring cup. If candy falls out of the spoon, he leaves it on the floor.

6. That player goes back to his team and gives the next player the spoon to repeat the process.

7. After five minutes, the team with the most candy in its measuring cup wins!

WASHINGTON CROSSING THE POTOMAC (K-6)

SUPPLIES

Poster board

Assorted colors of construction paper

Glue

Scissors

Masking tape

8 ½ x 11-inch copy of Washington Dollar (one per child)

George Washington's real hair color was red, and he was the only President who did not live in The White House.

DIRECTIONS

1. Make a Potomac River scene on the poster board with construction paper and glue.

2. Place the Potomac River on the floor about 3 feet from the players.

3. Make a line for them to stand behind with the masking tape.

4. Each child gets a copy of the Washington Dollar. Instruct them to fold their bills into paper airplanes and put their names on them.

5. Have the players, one at a time, make their journeys across the Potomac River (flying their planes). Their planes need to go over the water. The child whose plane goes the farthest wins!

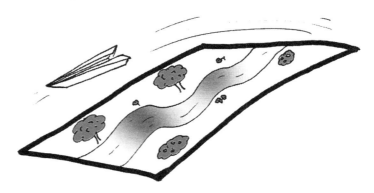

FAST BLAST VALENTINE TOSS (K-6)

SUPPLIES

Empty display box used to hold tall clear tubes of candy such as M&M's® (ask for the boxes at discount stores)

Masking tape

Seven ping-pong balls (in a container)

DIRECTIONS

1. Place the empty display box on the floor.

2. Mark a starting line with the masking tape about 3 feet from the box. Adjust the distance if needed.

3. Give the players, one at a time, seven ping-pong balls to toss at the box. For each ball that lands and stays in a hole, the player scores 2 points. The goal is to get 14 points to represent February 14th, Valentine's Day.

4. After all the children have played once, quit or continue playing if time permits.

What part makes a school Valentine Party fun?

"Good treats, and fun games."

Adam Rowan, Age 9½

FEBRUARY & PRESIDENTS' GAMES

VALENTINE STATIC (K-6)

SUPPLIES

Scissors

Red tissue paper

Blown-up balloons (one per child)

DIRECTIONS

1. Before hand, cut out lots of hearts from the tissue paper.

2. Spread the hearts onto the floor.

3. Have the children rub the balloons on their hair and then use them to pick up the hearts. This works great!

Note: If you have rotating groups, you can have less balloons. But be aware that after so many uses, the balloons might lose their static ability.

Tip: Have a few extra balloons in case they pop.

SUPPLIES FOR FEBRUARY & PRESIDENTS' GAMES

CALENDAR TOSS (K-6)

- 22 x 28-inch white poster board
- Black permanent marker
- Red permanent marker
- Three 2-inch wooden hearts (found at craft stores)
- Masking tape

LINCOLN'S HAT PENNY DROP (K-6)

- Two 9 x 12-inch sheets black construction paper
- Tape
- Empty oatmeal container
- Knife
- Pennies (six per child)

HUMAN VALENTINE TIC-TAC-TOE (1-6)

- Red permanent marker
- 6 x 6-inch square plain white paper (one per child)
- Masking tape (or chalk if played outside)

VALENTINE CANDY RELAY (K-6)

- Masking tape
- Two spoons
- Two bowls
- Two bags of small Valentine candy
- Two 2-cup measuring cups

WASHINGTON CROSSING THE POTOMAC (K-6)

- Poster board
- Assorted colors of construction paper
- Glue
- Scissors
- Masking tape
- 8½ x 11-inch copy of Washington Dollar (one per child)

FAST BLAST VALENTINE TOSS (K-6)

- Empty display box used to hold tall clear tubes of candy such as M&M's® (ask for the boxes at discount stores)
- Masking tape
- Seven ping-pong balls (in a container)

VALENTINE STATIC (K-6)

- Scissors
- Red tissue paper
- Blown-up balloons (one per child)

Don't forget the camera and film.

ALL-TIME FAVORITE GAMES

VALENTINE BINGO (K-4)

SUPPLIES
Pink copy paper
Red crayons, pencils or markers (one per student)
Prizes (one per student)

This is a Bingo game in which the whole class will Bingo at the same time. Keep this a secret! Read Tips 1 to 3 before playing.

DIRECTIONS

1. Make pink copies of the Valentine Bingo cards on the previous pages, using all five variations.

2. Each child gets a crayon and a Bingo card.

3. Explain to the class that when a number is called out, they should cross out that number if it is on their card. Tell them that they are playing diagonal Bingo. Show them what this means by demonstrating it on the blackboard. This is important if the game is to work the correct way.

4. Tell them when they get a diagonal bingo to yell "BINGO!"

5. Read the numbers from left to right, starting with the first line, then go to the second line and read from left to right and so on. They must be read in this order. The numbers that are colored with asterisks are the winning Bingo numbers. When the last number is called everyone will be yelling "BINGO!"

B-7	N-32	G-50	*I-29	B-13	O-74	G-47
O-71	I-19	N-36	*B-8	G-55	N-42	I-20
B-4	G-53	O-61	B-12	I-21	N-43	O-63
*N-40	B-6	B-1	I-30	N-44	G-46	*O-75
I-16	*G-49					

Tip 1: Some children are very wise (especially the older ones) and wonder why you're not reaching into a container to pull out Bingo balls or chips. Trick them by creating bingo chips that you are pretending to read (you really are reading from a list). You also can put letters and numbers on the Bingo chips, but they would have to be pulled out so you read the numbers in the order listed above.

Tip 2: If other classes are playing this game, and classroom doors are open, your class may catch on to them all screaming "Bingo" at the same time. So keep the doors closed.

Tip 3: Do not play this Bingo game every year. Some children remember it and tell the secret, ruining the surprise for others.

What does Valentine's Day mean to you?
"Getting Valentine cards that come with candy."
Kelly Hill, Age 8

Valentine School Parties

ALL-TIME FAVORITE GAMES

B	I	N	G	O
8	16	45	46	65
9	29	39	60	66
15	17	40	59	67
4	18	32	49	71
1	20	33	48	75

B	I	N	G	O
8	18	41	50	74
12	29	39	51	70
3	25	40	48	62
7	28	38	49	64
6	20	33	59	75

VALENTINE BINGO CARD

B	I	N	G	O
8	20	31	59	62
11	29	34	46	64
1	23	40	48	71
4	16	42	49	73
15	28	44	51	75

B	I	N	G	O
8	30	36	47	70
7	29	38	50	61
9	21	40	53	63
10	22	42	49	64
14	18	45	54	75

63

VALENTINE BINGO CARD

B	I	N	G	O
8	17	32	60	72
14	29	37	59	70
2	28	40	48	63
1	27	44	49	65
5	16	41	47	75

VALENTINE CONCENTRATION (1-6)

SUPPLIES

Assorted colors of construction paper

Scissors

Pictures (seven pairs of identical pictures)

Glue

Poster board or foam board

Red construction paper

Black permanent marker

Handi-Tak® (reusable adhesive)

Creativity (allow time to have fun with this one)

DIRECTIONS

1. Create a secret Valentine message (rebus) using pictures made from the assorted colors of construction paper. Glue your message to the board. If you are making a generic Valentine message which could be used another year, save it on foam board.

2. Make 15 paper blocks using red construction paper (see Tip #1). Draw a heart in black on the outside of each piece of paper after folding them top to bottom. Glue a picture (see Tip #2) on the inside of 14 of the 15 blocks. On the 15th block write "Wild."

3. Using Handi-Tak®, randomly cover the pictures on the board with the folded papers. Then number the papers in black in the heart so the numbers read consecutively across the board.

4. Divide the class into two teams. Boys versus girls works well with this game. The teams do not have to have an even number of players.

5. Decide which team will go first and have them pick two of the numbers on the board (have a team captain announce the numbers). Lift up the paper flaps on the number the captain calls out. If the pictures match, the paper is removed, revealing a portion of the puzzle (rebus). This team can try to guess the phrase; but limit their time to 30 seconds.

6. If they do not guess the phrase, the other team chooses two numbers and the game continues until a team solves the phrase.

Note: Time frame for this game varies from 10 to 20 minutes, depending on the difficulty of the message.

Tip 1: It works well to have 15 folded cards to cover the board. You will need seven matching pictures and one Wild card.

Tip 2: If you have an Ellison® Letter Machine™ at school, use this to cut matching pictures.

Examples of messages:

1. Would you be mine? (see illustration)

2. You are a great teacher, Miss _____

3. Lettuce be Valentines, Mrs. _____

VALENTINE WORD SEARCH (K-6)

ALL-TIME FAVORITE GAMES

1. Animals
2. Be Mine
3. Be True
4. Broken Heart
5. Bow and Arrow
6. Candy
7. Cards
8. Chocolate
9. Conversation
10. Couples
11. Cupid
12. February
13. Flowers
14. Friends
15. Fortune
16. Fourteen
17. Gifts
18. Heart
19. Heartthrob
20. Honeybun
21. Hug
22. Huggable
23. I Love You
24. Kiss
25. Lace
26. Letters
27. Lincoln
28. Loveable
29. Love Birds
30. Lover's Knot
31. Mailbox
32. Married
33. Maybe
34. My Pal
35. Perfume
36. Pink
37. Post Office
38. Red
39. Rings
40. Romantic
41. Roses
42. Sweet
43. Sweetheart
44. Tradition
45. True Love
46. You're Cool
47. Valentine
48. Washington
49. Wedding
50. Wow

SUPPLIES
Copies of word search (one per child)
Pencils

DIRECTIONS

1. Make copies of the word search.
2. Explain to the children there are 50 hidden words. They might be spelled forward, backward, diagonally up or down.

C	Y	O	U	R	E	C	O	O	L	T	K	S	W	B
O	S	L	A	M	I	N	A	I	R	R	I	W	E	O
N	P	E	N	I	M	E	B	O	X	A	S	O	D	W
V	D	M	A	Y	B	E	R	I	T	D	E	W	D	A
E	M	A	I	L	B	O	X	N	R	I	C	T	I	N
R	O	M	A	N	T	I	C	U	A	T	I	V	N	D
S	H	B	E	M	S	A	O	B	E	I	F	A	G	A
A	V	U	R	Y	R	R	U	Y	H	O	F	L	R	R
T	O	R	G	D	E	I	P	E	T	N	O	E	O	R
I	L	B	S	X	T	N	L	N	E	L	T	N	S	O
O	S	W	E	E	T	G	E	O	E	S	S	T	E	W
N	A	J	U	I	E	S	S	H	W	D	O	I	S	A
C	H	O	C	O	L	A	T	E	S	R	P	N	E	S
H	E	F	R	N	A	O	I	R	T	I	C	E	M	H
U	A	O	N	O	C	U	V	M	U	B	A	E	U	I
B	R	U	T	S	E	K	Z	E	S	E	N	N	F	N
T	T	R	R	S	W	E	H	E	Y	V	D	U	R	G
O	T	T	A	R	P	L	U	V	G	O	Y	T	E	T
N	H	E	E	E	I	B	G	O	G	L	U	R	P	O
K	R	E	H	W	H	A	G	L	I	N	C	O	L	N
S	O	N	N	O	S	E	A	E	F	K	V	F	B	V
R	B	M	E	L	D	V	B	U	T	S	F	E	Z	S
E	C	Y	K	F	N	O	L	R	S	E	T	O	G	K
V	U	P	O	I	E	L	E	T	T	R	A	E	H	I
O	P	A	R	P	I	N	K	I	U	Z	I	Q	D	S
L	I	L	B	O	R	E	D	E	I	R	R	A	M	S
H	D	G	M	E	F	P	Y	R	A	U	R	B	E	F

HEART ATTACK (K-6)

SUPPLIES

Scissors (one per child)

Construction paper (Valentine colors)

Crayons or permanent markers

DIRECTIONS

1. Have the children think up a good deed that they can do for someone without that person knowing about it.

2. Have each child cut out a heart from construction paper.

3. The child will write down the following verse onto his heart and secretly deliver the heart after doing the good deed.

Optional: For younger children, have the verse written out for them and let them decorate their heart.

> Don't have a heart attack
> But when you turned your back
> A good deed I have done
> And you happened to be the one
> Happy Valentine's Day!

RED, RED, & MORE RED (2-6)

SUPPLIES

Lined paper

Pencils (one per child)

DIRECTIONS

1. Give everyone a piece of paper and pencil.

2. Allow them five minutes to write down as many red objects as they can think of.

3. The longest, legitimate list wins.

VALENTINE ICE CUBE MELT (K-6)

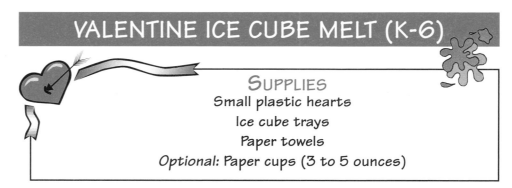

SUPPLIES
Small plastic hearts

Ice cube trays

Paper towels

Optional: Paper cups (3 to 5 ounces)

DIRECTIONS

1. Freeze plastic hearts in ice cubes.

2. Have the children form a circle and pass one heart ice cube around quickly.

   The object is not to be stuck with the heart when the ice has melted.

3. The child stuck with the heart is eliminated and stands back a little from the group.

4. The kids can melt a cube in about a minute, so have another one ready to go or use the option below.

Tip: Have paper towels ready to dry the children's wet hands.

Optional: Fill a few paper cups ½ to ¾ full. Place one plastic heart in each cup and freeze. Tear the paper cups off before using the "cubes." These larger ice cubes can take up to five minutes to melt in the children's hands, so you won't need as many.

What makes a school Valentine party fun?

"Getting Valentines."
Alyssa Ripple, Age 7

"Candy."
Rob Taylor, Age 8

SUPPLIES FOR ALL-TIME FAVORITE GAMES

VALENTINE BINGO (K-4)

- Pink copy paper
- Red crayons, pencils or markers (one per student)
- Prizes (one per student)

VALENTINE CONCENTRATION (1-6)

- Assorted colors of construction paper
- Scissors
- Pictures (seven pairs of identical pictures)
- Glue
- Poster board or foam board
- Red construction paper
- Black permanent marker
- Handi-Tak® (reusable adhesive)
- Creativity (allow time to have fun with this)

VALENTINE WORD SEARCH (K-6)

- Copies of word search (one per child)
- Pencils

HEART ATTACK (K-6)

- Scissors (one per child)
- Construction paper (Valentine colors)
- Crayons or permanent markers

RED, RED AND MORE RED (2-6)

- Lined paper
- Pencil (one per child)

VALENTINE ICE CUBE MELT (K-6)

- Small plastic hearts
- Ice cube trays
- Paper towels
- *Optional:* Paper cups (3 to 5 ounces)

Don't forget the camera and film.

CHAPTER THREE
HEARTS, CRAFTS & FAVORS

HELPFUL HINTS

HELPFUL HINTS FOR HEARTS, CRAFTS & FAVORS

1. Each idea in this section makes one craft. Children can make them, but may need some assistance from parents.

2. Substitute a craft for a game. Limit total craft time to 10 to 15 minutes. The children can complete most of the crafts in this allotted time, but if you feel you'll be short on time, prepare most of the steps before the party.

3. Watch for 50% off coupons and/or other great sales. Also, many stores offer school discounts, so be sure to ask!

4. Use newspaper, construction paper, and/or an old cut-up tablecloth (plastic or cloth) for mats. Children can work on these, leaving less mess for parents and themselves. Have the children help with clean-up.

5. Pre-cut items for younger children before the party.

6. Challenge the older grades with more detailed crafts.

7. A toothpick, instead of a pencil, can be used to trace onto craft foam.

8. Use static-cling window decorations to stick onto favor bags (with slick coating). If you stick them on that morning they will stay on all day. Glue them to stay longer.

9. Save lids from jars. When using glue, pour small amounts into them, one per child or one per small group.

10. Where a glue gun is recommended, you may substitute and use tacky glue, but be sure to allow enough drying time.

11. Make the crafts at the beginning of the party, or send them home the next day.

12. *Always, always* have a parent helper supervise when children are using a glue gun.

13. If crafts need time to dry, place them on paper plates marked with the children's names.

14. Ask the children to stay in their seats while making crafts, and tell them to raise their hands for help.

15. Younger children use their imagination to create, so don't over-pressure them with directions.

16. Encourage the older children to let their imaginations take over.

17. When supplies are limited, remind the children it's important to take turns and share.

18. A paper fastener is also called a brad.

19. Poster board is also called tag board.

20. February is National Children's Dental Health Month. To celebrate, set up a station and read a Tooth Fairy story to the children. Then give each child a Tooth Fairy pillow, page 102. To really make this a special event, have the storyteller dress like the Tooth Fairy. Ask your dentist to donate toothbrushes, toothpaste, and floss to include with each Tooth Fairy pillow.

HEART CRAFTS & FAVORS

PUZZLE HEART WREATH (K-6)

SUPPLIES

Red spray paint	Cardboard	*Optional: Glitter, beads, and assorted trinkets*
Puzzle pieces	Tacky glue	
Scissors	Picture hanger	

DIRECTIONS

1. Spray paint the puzzle pieces a couple of days before your party.
2. Cut the cardboard into a heart shape. Then, cut out the center of the wreath.
3. Glue the puzzle pieces onto the cardboard heart one layer at a time, until you're happy with your design.
4. Allow the heart to dry. Then attach the picture hanger to the back.

Optional: Decorate the finished wreath with glitter, beads, and trinkets.

Variation: You may choose to use the puzzles pieces "as is," without spray painting them, especially if they have Valentine colors or unique designs.

HEART SPOOL GAME FAVOR (K-6)

SUPPLIES

5-inch square piece of wood	Red acrylic paint	Sandwich bag
White acrylic paint	Sponge	15 inches red curling ribbon
Paintbrush	Hammer	Black permanent marker
Fourteen wooden spools	Fifteen small nails	

Mary likes Scott,
Susie likes Keith –
Good friends together
Make a Puzzle Heart Wreath

Karen Timm

DIRECTIONS

1. Paint one side of the wood white and let it dry.
2. Paint the spools red and let them dry.
3. Sponge a red heart onto the white side of the board, almost as wide as the board but leaving approximately an inch at the top.
4. Hammer the nails inside the heart in a triangle shape. Start with five nails on the top row, then four nails on the second row, then three nails, then two, and then one nail on the bottom row.
5. Enclose the spools in the bag, secure with the ribbon, and cut off any extra plastic.
6. Use the black marker to write **Jump the Spool** on the board above the heart.

JUMP THE SPOOL

To Play

1. Place the spools on the nails, except the middle nail of the third row.
2. Jump one spool over another, removing the jumped spool off the board. You may only jump over one spool at a time.
3. The object of the game: Jump spools until you have only one left. Keep trying. It can be done!

HANGING BEADED HEART (1-6)

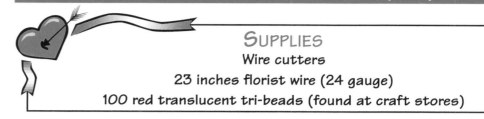

SUPPLIES

Wire cutters

23 inches florist wire (24 gauge)

100 red translucent tri-beads (found at craft stores)

DIRECTIONS

1. Cut the wire so you have a 16-inch piece and a 7-inch piece.

2. Thread the beads onto the 16-inch wire.

3. Twist one end of the wire around the other end to secure, leaving no space between the beads.

4. Form the long wire and the beads into a heart. Attach and shape the 7-inch wire to form a hanging hook, with the hook at the top.

5. Cut off any excess wire.

Note: Younger children may require help twisting the wires and using the wire cutters.

HEART PINWHEEL (K-3)

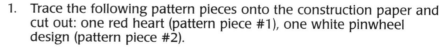

SUPPLIES

Pencil	White construction paper	Red push pin
2½-inch square red construction paper	Scissors	Straw
	Red-colored pencil	½-inch square piece of cork

DIRECTIONS

1. Trace the following pattern pieces onto the construction paper and cut out: one red heart (pattern piece #1), one white pinwheel design (pattern piece #2).

2. On the pinwheel design draw the dotted lines, dots in the corners, large circle in center, and hearts as shown on the pattern piece. Flip over, and draw only the dotted lines and hearts on the other side.

3. Color in all the hearts with the red-colored pencil.

4. Cut on the dotted lines, inward, toward the center, stopping at the large circle.

5. Take one dotted corner, curve it toward the large center circle and hold it with your other hand. Repeat with the other three dotted corners. Now your pinwheel has taken shape.

6. Place the red heart over the corners in the center, push the push pin through all, then through the end of the straw, and finally into the cork.

7. Slightly bend the front of the pinwheel forward from the center. This will allow it to turn better.

HEART PINWHEEL PATTERN

#1

#2

75

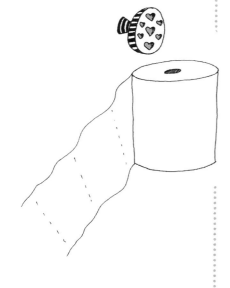

HEART CRAFTS & FAVORS

VALENTINE LACED CANDY HEART (K-6)

SUPPLIES

Scissors

Red construction paper

Pen

Clear vinyl

Paper hole puncher

Tape

Red yarn

Conversation heart candy

DIRECTIONS

1. Cut out a five-inch heart from the red construction paper.

2. Trace the red heart onto the vinyl and cut out.

3. Lay the vinyl heart on top of the construction heart and punch holes every $1/2$ inch along the edges, about $1/4$ inch in from the edges.

4. Wind a small piece of tape onto one end of the yarn. This will be the end you pull through the holes in the hearts.

5. To lace both hearts together, start at the top and pull the taped end of the yarn through one hole, leaving about 2 inches of yarn loose to secure a bow. Continue sewing until you get approximately 2 inches from the top. The stitches will loop around the edge of the heart.

6. Keeping the heart-pouch flat, fill it with candy. Be careful not to overflow it.

7. Finish lacing the heart until you reach the starting point, and tie both ends of the yarn into a bow. Snip off the taped end.

TOILET PAPER HEARTS (K-6)

SUPPLIES

One roll of toilet paper

Small clay heart cookie stamp

Water

Tacky glue

3 x 4-inch mat board (any color)

Makes a nice gift!

DIRECTIONS

1. Lay one sheet of toilet paper across the clay part of the cookie stamp.

2. Dampen the toilet paper with water, pressing down on the edges of the stamp.

3. Lay another sheet of toilet paper on top of the damp paper and once again, dampen with water.

4. Repeat the process five more times.

5. Press down along the edge of the stamp on the layers of toilet paper. Slowly tear off the excess paper, and discard.

6. Carefully peel the toilet paper off the mold. Turn over and let dry about one day.

7. Center and glue the toilet paper heart design onto the mat board.

Note: Occasionally the toilet paper design may start curling at the edges after drying a few hours. If this happens lay a book across it to keep it flat as it dries.

SUPPLIES FOR HEART CRAFTS & FAVORS

PUZZLE HEART WREATH (K-6)
- Red spray paint
- Puzzle pieces
- Scissors
- Cardboard
- Tacky glue
- Picture hanger
- Optional: Glitter, beads, and assorted trinkets

HEART SPOOL GAME FAVOR (K-6)
- 5-inch square piece of wood
- White acrylic paint
- Paintbrush
- Fourteen wooden spools
- Red acrylic paint
- Sponge
- Hammer
- Fifteen small nails
- Sandwich bag
- 15 inches red curling ribbon
- Black permanent marker

HANGING BEADED HEART (1-6)
- Wire cutters
- 23 inches florist wire (24 gauge)
- 100 red translucent tri-beads (found at craft stores)

HEART PINWHEEL (K-3)
- Pencil
- 2½-inch square red construction paper
- White construction paper
- Scissors
- Red-colored pencil
- Red push pin
- Straw
- ½-inch square piece of cork

VALENTINE LACED CANDY HEART (K-6)
- Scissors
- Red construction paper
- Pen
- Clear vinyl
- Paper hole puncher
- Tape
- Red yarn
- Conversation heart candy

TOILET PAPER HEARTS (K-6)
- One roll of toilet paper
- Small clay heart cookie stamp
- Water
- Tacky glue
- 3 x 4-inch mat board (any color)

CUPID CRAFTS & FAVORS

CUPID BOOKMARK (K-4)

SUPPLIES

Pencil

4¹/₂ x 5¹/₂-inch pink craft foam

1¹/₂ x 4-inch white craft foam

Scissors

Curly blond craft hair

Glue gun

Red permanent marker

Black permanent marker

Powdered blush (dark color)

Toothpick

Cellophane frills toothpick (any color)

5 inches gold craft wire

Tongue depressor

DIRECTIONS

1. Trace the following pattern pieces onto the craft foam and cut out: one pink Cupid (pattern piece #1), one white wing (pattern piece #2), and two white arrow tips (pattern piece #3).

2. Cut pieces of hair, glue on the top of Cupid's head, and let dry.

3. Draw and color a heart-mouth using the red permanent marker.

4. Draw a heart for each eye with the black permanent marker. Color smaller hearts within the larger hearts to represent Cupid's pupils.

5. Rub the tip of your finger onto the blush then onto Cupid's cheeks.

6. Use the red permanent marker to draw and color shorts on Cupid.

7. Form Cupid's bow and arrow, gluing the regular toothpick on top of the cellophane frills toothpick in an X shape. Let dry.

8. Wrap one end of the wire on one end of the regular toothpick, and the other end of the wire onto the other end. Form the wire into an arc away from the frilled end of the cellophane toothpick.

9. Glue the arrow points (pattern #3) together, inserting the non-frilled end of the toothpick into the base of the arrow point.

10. Bring Cupid's arms together, placing the bow and arrow between them at the X so the wire and arrow point are in front of the arms, and the regular toothpick is vertical. Glue the arms and bow and arrow together, with the arms overlapped enough to "hold" the bow and arrow.

11. Glue the wings (pattern #2) on the back of Cupid's shoulders.

12. Glue one end of the tongue depressor to Cupid's back.

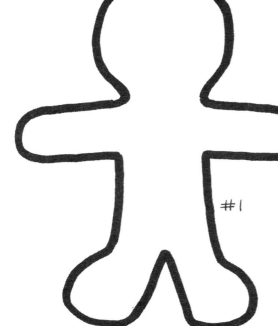

#1

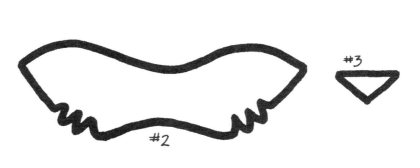

#3

#2

78

BOW & ARROW CANDY (K-6)

SUPPLIES

Electric drill with ³/₁₆" bit

½ inch thick small wooden heart

Red paint

Paint brush

Wax paper

6 inches ³/₁₆" wooden dowel

Roll of cherry Lifesavers®

Glue gun

2½ x 4½-inch silver mylar paper

2½ x 4½-inch red mylar paper

Scissors

Optional: Heart-shaped eraser instead of wooden heart

DIRECTIONS

1. Drill a hole in the top of the wooden heart about ³/₈ inch deep, as if headed towards the tip.

2. Paint one side of the heart and lay it on wax paper to dry. Then paint the opposite side of the heart and its edges. Paint a second and third coat if needed.

3. Insert the wooden dowel through the center of the Lifesaver's® roll.

4. Glue one end of the dowel into the hole in the heart.

5. Lay the silver mylar paper on top of the red mylar paper and fold both in half to measure 2¼ x 2½-inches. Cut the mylar paper every ⅛ inch toward the fold to about ½ inch from the fold. This will create the feathers of the arrow.

6. Place the mylar paper underneath the end of the dowel opposite the heart, with the folded edge closest to the Lifesavers® candy.

7. Glue one corner of the folded end of the mylar onto the dowel and quickly wrap the mylar around the dowel, gluing to secure it.

Optional: You may use an eraser for the arrow point in place of the wooden heart.

CUPID COASTERS (K-6)

SUPPLIES

Scissors

Corkboard

Rubber cement

Old Valentines with Cupids (or greeting cards)

Polyurethane

Brushes

DIRECTIONS

1. Cut two 3-inch squares out of the corkboard.

2. Glue the pieces of cork together using the rubber cement.

3. Cut a Cupid from a Valentine to fit on top of the coaster.

4. Glue the Cupid in place.

5. Seal the Cupid with polyurethane. Make several and let dry.

The United States Post Office has these tips for writing letters: Write letters on fresh, clean stationery, use neat handwriting, keep a dictionary handy, spell words correctly, and always answer your mail. If you are too little to write, ask your Mom or Dad to help you.

CUPID'S MINI QUIVER (K-6)

SUPPLIES

Can opener
6-ounce empty juice can
Pliers
Red construction paper
Scissors
Tacky glue

6-inch red metallic cord
Three sugar-filled straws
Assorted Valentine candy and trinkets
Optional: Black permanent marker

DIRECTIONS

1. Cut the lid off the can, pinching down any sharp edges with pliers. Wash and dry the can thoroughly.

2. Fit red construction paper around the can, trim, and glue in place.

3. Glue one end of the metallic cord (quiver strap) to the top of the can on the inside, and the other end to the bottom.

4. Cut three 2½ x 4½-inch strips out of the red construction paper.

5. Fold each in half to measure 2¼ x 2½ inches. Cut every ⅛-inch toward the fold to about ½ inch away from the fold. This will create the feathers of an arrow.

6. Glue the folded edge of the feathers onto one end of a sugar-filled straw and quickly wind around the straw, gluing to secure. Repeat steps 5 and 6 two more times.

7. Fill the can (quiver) with Valentine candy, trinkets, and the three sugar-filled straw arrows.

Optional: Personalize the can with the child's name, such as "Angela's Quiver."

CUPID STATIONERY (K-6)

SUPPLIES

Cupid stamp
Stamp pad (any color)

Three sheets plain stationery paper with envelopes (any color)

Colored markers
12 inches ribbon (any color)

Makes one set

DIRECTIONS

1. Set up a station for the children to create their own set of Cupid stationery. Put all the supplies on a table.

2. Let the children stamp a Cupid on three pieces of stationery and envelopes however they choose, but they need to leave the address areas on the envelopes blank.

3. They then add any additional decorations to their stationery and envelopes using markers.

4. Have them fold their stationery to fit into their envelopes, but not place them in the envelopes.

5. They then place their stationery on top of their envelopes, wrap their ribbons around their sets, and tie in bows.

Note: Adjust the ribbon length if needed according to the envelope size. Each child's set should be uniform, but does not have to be the same size as the other children's sets.

SUPPLIES FOR CUPID CRAFTS & FAVORS

CUPID BOOKMARK (K-4)

- Pencil
- 4½ x 5½-inch pink craft foam
- 1½ x 4-inch white craft foam
- Scissors
- Curly blond craft hair
- Glue gun
- Red permanent marker
- Black permanent marker
- Powdered blush (dark color)
- Toothpick
- Cellophane frills toothpick (any color)
- 5 inches gold craft wire
- Tongue depressor

BOW & ARROW CANDY (K-6)

- Electric drill with $^3/_{16}$" bit
- ½ inch thick small wooden heart
- Red paint
- Paint brush
- Wax paper
- 6 inches $^3/_{16}$" wooden dowel
- Roll of cherry Lifesavers®
- Glue gun
- 2½ x 4½-inch silver mylar paper
- 2½ x 4½-inch red mylar paper
- Scissors
- *Optional: Heart-shaped eraser instead of wooden heart*

CUPID COASTERS (K-6)

- Scissors
- Corkboard
- Rubber cement
- Old Valentines with Cupids (or greeting cards)
- Polyurethane
- Brushes

CUPID'S MINI QUIVER (K-6)

- Can opener
- 6-ounce empty juice can
- Pliers
- Red construction paper
- Scissors
- Tacky glue
- 6-inch red metallic cord
- Three sugar-filled straws
- Assorted Valentine candy and trinkets
- *Optional: Black permanent marker*

CUPID STATIONERY (K-6)

- Cupid stamp
- Stamp pad (any color)
- Three sheets plain stationery paper with envelopes (any color)
- Colored markers
- 12 inches ribbon (any color)

LOVE & FRIENDSHIP CRAFTS & FAVORS

KING & QUEEN CROWNS (K-3)

SUPPLIES

Scissors	Heart stickers
4 x 24-inch white poster board	Stapler
	Optional: Crayons

DIRECTIONS

1. Cut crown points in one edge of the poster board strip.
2. Lay flat, and to your own liking, place heart stickers onto the crown.
3. Staple ends of the poster board to form a crown, using your head for measuring if needed.

Optional: Children can decorate their crowns using crayons, and personalize them with their names, such as "King Quinn" or "Queen Diana."

CANDY ROSE (K-6)

SUPPLIES

Two Hershey's Kisses®	Red cellophane wrap
25 inches green floral tape	Artificial stem

DIRECTIONS

1. Hold the two Hershey's Kisses® flat sides together.
2. Smoothly and tightly wrap the piece of cellophane over the tip of one of the kisses and down over the other kiss. Twist the excess cellophane below the tip of the second kiss.
3. Lay the stem on top of the excess cellophane and hold snugly.
4. Start wrapping the floral tape around the stem and cellophane just beneath the kisses, inserting the artificial leaf near the top of the stem. Continue wrapping the tape down the stem, overlapping it and pulling it tight, until you reach the bottom. Tear off excess tape.
5. Tie a bow from the ribbon just beneath the leaf.

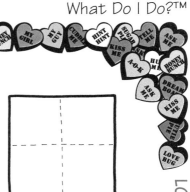

PAPER FORTUNE TELLER (K-6)

SUPPLIES
7-inch square piece of plain paper (any color)
Red permanent marker

DIRECTIONS

1. Fold the paper in half one way, then open it up and fold it again in the opposite direction, being sure to crease the folds well.

2. Open it up, and fold the tip of each corner to the center, creasing the new folds as well.

3. Flip the paper over and fold the new corners to the center again. With this new square, repeat Step #1.

4. Now you have four sections with two triangles each. Going around the square, number the triangles 1 through 8.

5. Open up each section and write a fortune on each triangle, a total of eight fortunes.

6. Close the sections and flip the paper over again. Write a name of a color on each of the four squares.

7. Fold the paper in half, and insert your thumb and middle finger from one hand underneath two squares on one side of the fold. Repeat for the other side with the other hand.

8. To tell a person's fortune, have him pick a color, open and close the Fortune Teller with your finger the amount of times it takes to spell out the color. For example, open and close the Fortune Teller three times while repeating the letters "R E D."

9. Next, have him choose one of the numbers. Open and close the Fortune Teller according to the number that he chooses. For example, four times for the number "4."

10. Repeat Step #9 again.

11. Have him choose a number for a third time. Lift up the triangle that displays the chosen number. Read his fortune.

Examples of fortunes:

* You will marry at age 18.

* Good luck will come in the mail.

* You will get an "A" on your test.

* You will find some money.

* You will meet a new friend.

* On Saturday, you will do something fun.

* It's time to do a good deed.

* Think before you act.

Note: Some children prefer to choose numbers only once, therefore eliminating Step #10.

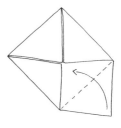

Frontview

Backview

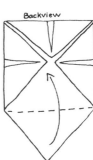

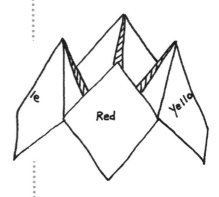

Red

FRIENDSHIP BRACELETS (1-6)

SUPPLIES
Tape

Six 12-inch plastic metallic cords (different colors)

DIRECTIONS

1. Choose a friend to make and exchange bracelets with. (Parents may wish to choose partners so that no one feels left out.) Tape down the ends of three cords onto a flat surface.

2. Braid the cords tightly until you get to the end.

3. Remove the tape carefully, holding onto both ends of the bracelet. Wrap the bracelet around your friend's wrist, and tie the ends together in a double knot.

4. Cut off any excess.

5. Using the remaining three cords, your friend can make a bracelet for you.

Note: Younger children may need help with the braiding unless their partners can help them.

CANDY FIT FOR A KING & QUEEN (K-6)

SUPPLIES

Scissors

Red craft foam

Glue gun

Two 6-inch pieces of red pipe cleaner

One King and one Queen of Hearts playing cards

Styrofoam® base

Two Valentine suckers

Assorted wrapped Valentine candy

Straight pins

DIRECTIONS

1. Cut four ½-inch hearts from the craft foam. Glue one heart onto each end of the pipe cleaner pieces.

2. Glue one pipe cleaner piece horizontally behind each card to form arms. Bend the arms forward.

3. Place the playing cards side-by-side and angling out into the Styrofoam® base. Link the King and Queen's arms by bending one pipe cleaner around the other.

4. Place the Valentine suckers into the Styrofoam® base, one at each end so one is to the left of one card, and the other is to the right of the other card.

5. Place assorted Valentine candy on the Styrofoam® base around the cards, and secure them with the pins.

84

SEEDS FOR FRIENDSHIP (K-6)

SUPPLIES

Galvanized water can (found at craft stores)

Red acrylic paint

Wax paper

Small heart sponge

Paper towel

Red or white shredded paper

Package of garden seeds (Zinnia for "friends" and Forget-Me-Nots for "true love")

1 x 2-inch card stock

Black permanent marker

Paper hole puncher

6 inches red curling ribbon

Scissors

Optional: Assorted colors of acrylic paint and paint brushes

DIRECTIONS

1. Wash and dry the can.

2. Squeeze a small amount of paint onto the wax paper.

3. Dip the heart sponge into the paint and then lightly sponge onto the paper towel a couple of times. This will help remove any excess paint.

4. Sponge heart shapes onto your can and let dry.

5. Place the shredded paper inside the can and place a package of seeds upright into the can.

6. Write "Seeds for Friendship" or "Seeds for Love" on the card stock with the permanent marker. Punch a hole into the corner of the card and tie the curling ribbon on the card. Curl the ribbon with the scissors and then tie the ribbon to the can's handle.

Optional: Get creative and paint the can to your liking.

What does Valentine's Day mean to you?

"Candy and friends."
Cassie Mason, Age 6

"Valentine Party."
Sean and Theresa Ayers, Ages 10 and 9

SUPPLIES FOR LOVE & FRIENDSHIP CRAFTS & FAVORS

KING & QUEEN CROWNS (K-3)

Scissors

4 x 24-inch white poster board

Heart stickers

Stapler

Optional: Crayons

CANDY ROSE (K-6)

Two Hershey's Kisses®

25 inches green floral tape

Red cellophane wrap

Artificial stem

Artificial leaf

8 inches red ribbon

PAPER FORTUNE TELLER (K-6)

7-inch square piece of plain paper (any color)

Red permanent marker

FRIENDSHIP BRACELETS (1-6)

Tape

Six 12-inch plastic metallic cords (different colors)

CANDY FIT FOR A KING & QUEEN (K-6)

Scissors

Red craft foam

Glue gun

Two 6-inch pieces of red pipe cleaner

One King and one Queen of Hearts playing cards

Styrofoam® base

Two Valentine suckers

Assorted wrapped Valentine candy

Straight pins

SEEDS FOR FRIENDSHIP (K-6)

Galvanized water can (found at craft stores)

Red acrylic paint

Wax paper

Small heart sponge

Paper towel

Red or white shredded paper

Package of garden seeds (Zinnia for "friends" and Forget-Me-Nots for "true love")

1 x 2-inch card stock

Black permanent marker

Paper hole puncher

6 inches red curling ribbon

Scissors

Optional: Assorted colors of acrylic

ANIMAL CRAFTS & FAVORS

VALENTINE MOUSE (K-6)

SUPPLIES

Scissors

Two sheets pink construction paper

Tacky glue

6 inches gray yarn

Black permanent marker

3mm pink pom-pom (nose)

DIRECTIONS

1. Cut two miniature hearts, along with a small, medium, and large heart from the pink construction paper.

2. Fold the large heart in half. Glue the piece of gray yarn inside the heart at the fold opposite the tip. This is the mouse's tail.

3. Fold both miniature hearts in half and glue to the bottom of the mouse's body to create legs.

4. Cut a small slit about 1½-inches up from the tip of the folded heart and opposite the fold.

5. Use the black permanent marker to make a large dot right below the slit. This will be the mouse's eye.

6. Slide the tip of the smallest heart into the slit, to give the mouse ears.

7. Glue the pom-pom on the heart's tip for the nose.

8. On the medium-sized heart, write a fortune such as "You'll have a surprise today! Happy Valentine's Day!" Fold the heart in half, with the fortune on the outside, then slide it into the large heart.

BEE MINE VISOR (K-4)

SUPPLIES

Red plastic visor

Black paint marker

Optional: Bumblebee sticker

DIRECTIONS

1. Using the paint marker, draw hearts on the visor.

2. Write the words "Bee Mine" on the visor.

Optional: Place a bumblebee sticker onto the visor.

ANIMAL CRAFTS & FAVORS

Lovebirds are colorful parrots who perch in pairs.

Hearts are red,
Violets are blue,
Flying Lovebirds —
Great fun to do!

Karen Timm

FLYING LOVEBIRDS (K-6)

SUPPLIES

Pencil	Scissors	Paper hole puncher
6½ x 13-inch white craft foam	Tacky glue	Heavy string
2½ x 6½-inch red craft foam	Four 10mm moving eyes	Wooden dowel rod

DIRECTIONS

1. Trace the following pattern pieces onto the craft foam and cut out: two white lovebirds (pattern piece #1), four white wings (pattern piece #2), and twelve red hearts (pattern piece #3).

2. Glue a wing to each side of both lovebirds' bodies toward the back, with the round side up and the arched side just covering the top of the tail.

3. Glue the hearts on the lovebirds, two on the outer side of each wing, and one on each side of the bodies.

4. Glue one eye onto each side of the birds' heads.

5. Punch a hole at the top center of each bird. Thread strings through the holes and knot.

6. Then wrap the string around the wooden dowel, and tie securely. Your birds are ready to fly — just wave the dowel.

FEBRUARY BUTTERFLY (K-6)

SUPPLIES

Wooden clamp clothespin

Red acrylic paint

Paintbrush

Pencil

5-inch square red craft foam

2-inch square purple craft foam

2-inch square white craft foam

Scissors

Glue gun

4-inch red pipe cleaner

Lunch bag (any color)

Assorted Valentine candy and trinkets

DIRECTIONS

1. Paint the clothespin red, and let dry.

2. Trace the following pattern pieces from the craft foam and cut out: two red hearts (pattern piece #1), two red hearts (pattern piece #2), two purple hearts (pattern piece #3), four white hearts (pattern piece #3), four white hearts (pattern piece #4), two red hearts (pattern piece #4), and two purple hearts (pattern piece #4).

3. Glue the tips of the two largest red hearts (large wings) to the clothespin, one into each side of the clasping end (body).

4. Glue the tips of the second largest red hearts (small wings), one into each side of the bottom end of the clothespin (wings).

5. Glue the two purple hearts (pattern piece #3), one in the center of each large wing, tips pointed toward the clothespin.

6. Glue the four white hearts (pattern piece #3) to each outer edge of the large wings, with tips pointed toward the clothespin.

7. Glue the four smallest white hearts (pattern piece #4) to each outer edge of the small wings.

8. Bend the pipe cleaner in half to shape the antennae, and glue one of the smallest red hearts (pattern piece #4) onto the end of each antenna. Glue the antennae's "V" into the clasping end of the clothespin, so the antennae stick out.

9. Fill the lunch bag with an assortment of Valentine candy and trinkets.

10. Attach the clothespin to the top edge of the lunch bag.

#1

#2

#3

#4

89

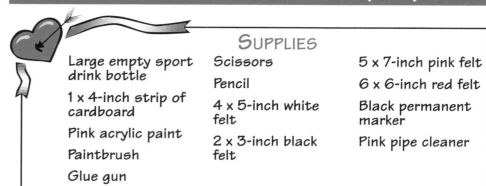

VALENTINE PIGGY BANK (K-4)

SUPPLIES

Large empty sport drink bottle

1 x 4-inch strip of cardboard

Pink acrylic paint

Paintbrush

Glue gun

Scissors

Pencil

4 x 5-inch white felt

2 x 3-inch black felt

5 x 7-inch pink felt

6 x 6-inch red felt

Black permanent marker

Pink pipe cleaner

DIRECTIONS

1. Rinse out the sport drink bottle and let it dry. Don't discard the cap.

2. Paint the cardboard pink, and let it dry.

3. Turn the bottle on its side and glue it onto the cardboard. The cardboard will help to stabilize the bottle (bank).

4. Using scissors, carefully cut a slit on the top of the bottle for money to slide in.

5. Trace the following pattern pieces onto the felt and cut out: two white eyes (pattern piece #1) two black pupils (pattern piece #2), two pink ears (pattern piece #3), one pink snout (pattern piece #4), and four red hearts (pattern piece #5).

6. Glue the pink snout on the bottle's cap. Use the permanent marker to dot nostrils on the snout.

7. Glue one white felt eye on each side of the pig's head, past the snout.

8. Glue the black pupils onto the white eyes.

9. Slightly crease the pink ears and glue one on each side of the head, just behind and above the eyes, and sticking up.

10. Wind the pipe cleaner around the pencil to curl it, then glue it onto the back of the piggy for its tail.

11. Glue the red hearts to the piggy bank where desired.

Optional: Personalize the bottle with the child's name, such as "Sheila's Piggy Bank."

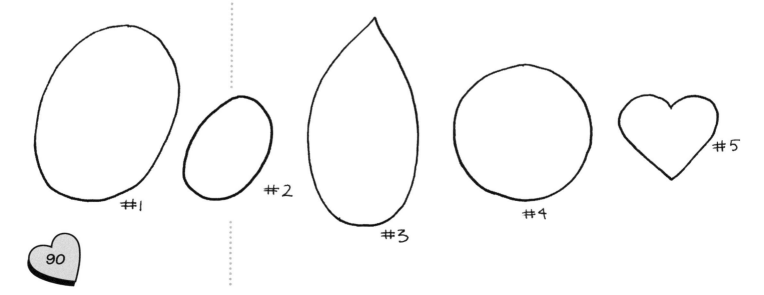

#1

#2

#3

#4

#5

DOVE GEOBOARD (K-6)

SUPPLIES

7 x 8-inch wooden board

White spray paint

Pencil

Hammer

Nineteen small nails

Five #16 rubber bands

DIRECTIONS

1. Pre-make the Geoboards giving directions to the children on how to hook and wrap the rubber bands.

2. Spray paint the block of wood white and let dry.

3. Lightly trace the dove pattern onto the board, marking the dotted areas.

4. Hammer the nails part way into the board at the dotted areas.

5. Follow the illustration showing how the nails are numbered, without writing the numbers. Pay close attention to the arrows showing the direction the rubber bands go around the nails.

6. The first rubber band hooks on nails 1 and 4, and wraps around the nails between. If it doesn't reach nail 4, you haven't pulled it tight enough.

7. The second rubber band hooks on nails 4 and 8, and wraps around nails 5, 6, and 7.

8. The third rubber band hooks on nails 8 and 12, the fourth rubber band hooks on nails 12 and 17, and the fifth rubber band hooks on nail 17, around 18 and 19, and then hooks onto nail 1.

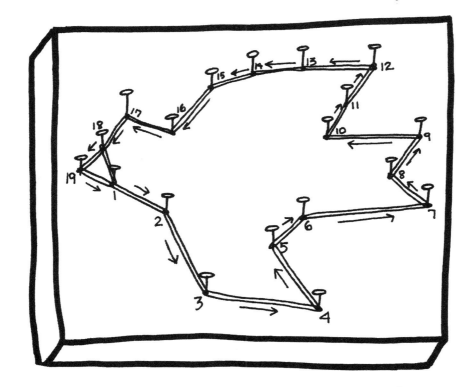

SUPPLIES FOR ANIMAL CRAFTS & FAVORS

VALENTINE MOUSE (K-6)

- Scissors
- Two sheets pink construction paper
- Tacky glue
- 6 inches gray yarn
- Black permanent marker
- 3mm pink pom-pom (nose)

BEE MINE VISOR (K-4)

- Red plastic visor
- Black paint marker
- *Optional: Bumblebee sticker*

FLYING LOVEBIRDS (K-6)

- Pencil
- 6½ x 13-inch white craft foam
- 2½ x 6½-inch red craft foam
- Scissors
- Tacky glue
- Four 10mm moving eyes
- Paper hole puncher
- Heavy string
- Wooden dowel rod

Don't forget the camera and film.

FEBRUARY BUTTERFLY (K-6)

- Wooden clamp clothespin
- Red acrylic paint
- Paintbrush
- Pencil
- 5-inch square red craft foam
- 2-inch square purple craft foam
- 2-inch square white craft foam
- Scissors
- Glue gun
- 4-inch red pipe cleaner
- Lunch bag (any color)
- Assorted Valentine candy and trinkets

VALENTINE PIGGY BANK (K-4)

- Large empty sport drink bottle
- 1 x 4-inch strip of cardboard
- Pink acrylic paint
- Paintbrush
- Glue gun
- Scissors
- Pencil
- 4 x 5-inch white felt
- 2 x 3-inch black felt
- 5 x 7-inch pink felt
- 6 x 6-inch red felt
- Black permanent marker
- Pink pipe cleaner

DOVE GEOBOARD (K-6)

- 7 x 8-inch wooden board
- White spray paint
- Pencil
- Hammer
- Nineteen small nails
- Five #16 rubber bands

POST OFFICE CRAFTS & FAVORS

CONVERSATION HEART SOAP SCULPTURE (4-6)

SUPPLIES

Toothpick

Bar of soap

Plastic knife

Hot water

DIRECTIONS

1. Using the toothpick, outline a heart shape on the soap. Leave a base for the heart to stand on.
2. Carve the shape out with the knife, being careful not to break the soap.
3. Using your finger, smooth out any rough edges with the hot water.

WOVEN MAIL BASKET (K-6)

SUPPLIES

2 yards Valentine ribbon

1 pint empty strawberry basket (cleaned)

Scissors

Glue gun

Three pipe cleaners

A tisket – a tasket
Weave a Mail Basket –
Send a Valentine,
Say that you'll be mine.
Karen Timm

DIRECTIONS

1. Weave the ribbon through the bottom row of the basket. Cut when done, leaving enough to glue to the other end of the ribbon.
2. Repeat the process with every row.
3. Twist the three pipe cleaners together at one end, and hook them to the top of the basket. Braid them tightly almost to the end.
4. Twist the end of the braid, and hook it to the opposite side of the basket. Now you have your handle, and a great basket for mailing your Valentines!

HOMEMADE VALENTINE STICKERS (K-6)

SUPPLIES

Scissors

Magazines

Popsicle® stick

1 tablespoon white vinegar

½ cup white glue

Paper bowl

DIRECTIONS

1. Cut assorted pictures out of the magazines.
2. Using the Popsicle® stick, mix the vinegar and glue together in the paper bowl.
3. Brush the mixture on the backside of the pictures. Place them on the wax paper, wet side up, and let them dry.
4. Lick your stickers to apply wherever you like.

Note: The longer you let the glue dry, the better your stickers will stick.

93

VALENTINE DIARY (2-6)

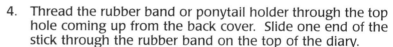

SUPPLIES

Scissors

13 x 18-inch black poster board

Twenty pieces 9 x 6½-inch sketch pad paper

Paper hole puncher

Thick rubber band or elastic ponytail holder

7 inches ¼" twig

Origami paper (found at craft stores)

Rubber cement

Optional: Embroidery floss, needle, and Valentine charms

DIRECTIONS

1. Cut the poster board in half to make two pieces measuring 9 x 6½ inches each.

2. Sandwich the sketch pad paper between the pieces of poster board, making a front cover, back cover, and inside pages.

3. On the left side of the journal, punch two holes into the poster board and paper (a few pieces at a time) approximately 1 inch from the top and the bottom, and ½ inch from the side. It works well to punch the holes in the poster board first, and then use it as a guide to punch your holes in the paper.

4. Thread the rubber band or ponytail holder through the top hole coming up from the back cover. Slide one end of the stick through the rubber band on the top of the diary.

5. Stretch the rubber band across the back cover, thread it through the other hole, and hook it onto the other end of the twig. Children may need help stretching the rubber band.

6. Cut the origami paper into heart shapes.

7. Glue the origami hearts onto the top of the journal.

8. Children can then write their Valentine memories from the party and include items such as photos and Valentine cards.*

Note: Be creative when choosing the paper. There are plenty of textured and speckled papers that would work great, but you may need to cut them to size.

Optional: Prick two small holes through the top cover. Thread the embroidery floss through the holes, attach and knot Valentine charms onto the floss. Knot the floss closed. Secure the charms by gluing them to the front cover.

*Refer to "Valentine Card Journal," created for younger children in K-1, in the All-Time Favorite Crafts & Favors section.

What does Valentine's Day mean to you?

"Getting and giving special cards with friends."

Adam Rowan, Age 9½

SECRET MAIL FAVOR (K-6)

SUPPLIES

Assorted small Valentine candy

5 x 7-inch manila envelope

Red washable inkpad

Red permanent marker

Rectangular-shaped Valentine stickers

DIRECTIONS

1. Place an assortment of candy into the envelope, and seal.

2. On the backside of the envelope, use the inkpad and your thumb to make a heart fingerprint as follows: press your thumb onto the inkpad and then onto the envelope, where it's sealed, angled to the left. Press the same thumb onto the inkpad and then onto the envelope again, but angled to the right. You will now have a heart shape.

3. Flip the envelope over to the front side and use the red permanent marker to address the envelope with a child's name, in care of the "name" of your school party. Make up a return address such as "Cupid, Heartland, USA."

4. Place a Valentine sticker where the stamp would be. Have a mailman come to the class to deliver it.

VALENTINE PICTURE POSTCARD (K-6)

SUPPLIES

22 x 28-inch white poster board

Pencil

Scissors

Permanent markers (assorted colors)

Polaroid camera and film

DIRECTIONS

1. Lay the poster board so the long sides are the top and bottom. Lightly draw and cut out a heart in the upper left-hand corner, large enough to frame a child's head. Above it write the word "From:" with black permanent marker. Children will stand behind the heart to have their picture taken.

2. Use the permanent markers to draw a stamp on the upper right hand corner. Write "To:" in the center of the poster board and three squiggly lines underneath to denote a name and address.

3. Have the child hold the poster board up, decorated side toward the camera, and fit his face into the heart cut-out. Snap the picture, wait until it develops, and give him his take-home Valentine picture postcard.

Send your Valentine a letter from one of these cute, romantic cities. Simply take it to your local post office weeks before Valentine's Day. They will then forward your letter to that city so that it can be mailed from that city marked with their cancellation.

Angels Camp, CA 95222
Loveland, CO 80538
Loveville, MD 26656
Loves Park, IL 61111
Loving, TX 75851
Valentine, TX 79854
Kissimmee, FL 34744
Rosebud, TX 76570
Sweet Home, OR 97386
Paradise Valley, AZ 85253
Hartville, WY 82215
Valentines, VA 23887
Lovingston, VA 20949
Loveland, OH 45140

POST OFFICE CRAFTS & FAVORS

SUPPLIES FOR POST OFFICE CRAFTS & FAVORS

CONVERSATION HEART SOAP SCULPTURE (4-6)

- Toothpick
- Bar of soap
- Plastic knife
- Hot water

WOVEN MAIL BASKET (K-6)

- 2 yards Valentine ribbon
- 1 pint empty strawberry basket (cleaned)
- Scissors
- Glue gun
- Three pipe cleaners (assorted colors)

HOMEMADE VALENTINE STICKERS (K-6)

- Scissors
- Magazines
- Popsicle® stick
- 1 tablespoon white vinegar
- 1/2 cup white glue
- Paper bowl
- Paint brush
- Wax paper

Don't forget the camera and film.

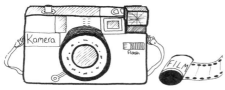

VALENTINE DIARY (2-6)

- Scissors
- 13 x 18-inch black poster board
- Twenty pieces 9 x 6½-inch sketch pad paper
- Paper hole puncher
- Thick rubber band or elastic ponytail holder
- 7 inches ¼" twig
- Origami paper (found at craft stores)
- Rubber cement
- *Optional:* Embroidery floss, needle, and Valentine charms

SECRET MAIL FAVOR (K-6)

- Assorted small Valentine candy
- 5 x 7-inch manila envelope
- Red washable inkpad
- Red permanent marker
- Rectangular-shaped Valentine stickers

VALENTINE PICTURE POSTCARD (K-6)

- 22 x 28-inch white poster board
- Pencil
- Scissors
- Permanent markers (assorted colors)
- Polaroid camera and film

FEBRUARY & PRESIDENTS' CRAFTS & FAVORS

SWEET SMELLING CHERRY PIE (K-6)

SUPPLIES

Potpourri (cherry scent)

9-inch disposable pie pan

9 x 9-inch light brown
cotton fabric

Zigzag scissors

Glue gun

DIRECTIONS

1. Empty the potpourri into the pie pan.

2. Cut the fabric with zigzag scissors into twelve 3/4-inch strips.

3. Lay half of the strips across the potpourri and glue to the edge of the pie pan. Lay the other strips in the opposite direction, securing the same way.

4. Going around the edge of the pie pan, cut off any excess fabric.

Note: You can weave your fabric strips by gluing one end to the edge of the pan and then glue the other end after you weave the strips.

Variation: Use a tart pan instead of the pie pan for a smaller Sweet Smelling Cherry Pie.

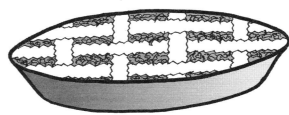

Lincoln and Washington,
Two presidents great —
Come February Fourteen,
Let's Celebrate!

Karen Timm

LOG CABIN KIT (K-6)

SUPPLIES

Pretzel rods

Bread knife

Canned chocolate frosting

Butter knife

5-inch square heavy mat board (neutral color)

5 x 8-inch brown poster board

Rectangular butter cookie

Heart-shaped candy

DIRECTIONS

1. Cut the pretzel rods in half using the bread knife.

2. With the frosting and butter knife, secure one pretzel rod to the edge of one side of the mat board. Then secure another rod on the opposite side.

3. Place a dab of frosting on the top of each pretzel's end. Add the second layer of logs by placing two pretzels' ends in the dabs of frosting, perpendicular to the first layer. Repeat until you reach your desired height.

4. Fold the poster board widthwise and frost it to the top of the cabin for a roof. The eaves should overlap the right and left sides slightly.

5. For the front door, glue the cookie on with frosting. Glue the heart-shaped candy on the cookie for the door handle. Let everything dry.

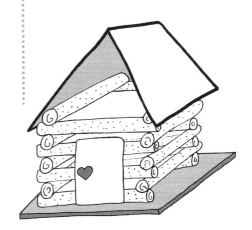

97

VALENTINE ROSE PEN (K-6)

SUPPLIES

Egg-shaped Styrofoam® ball	Artificial rose
Knife	Glue gun
Small clay pot	25 inches green floral tape
Bic® pen (any color)	Craft moss
Scissors	6 inches 1/8" red ribbon

DIRECTIONS

1. Cut a small tip off the Styrofoam® ball with the knife.

2. Push the Styrofoam® ball into the clay pot, flat end down.

3. Push the pen into the Styrofoam® ball, past the metal writing tip. At an angle, rotate it a few times to make a hole slightly larger than the pen. Be careful not to make the hole too large, as the hole will serve to hold the pen upright later. Remove the pen from the hole.

4. Use the scissors to force or cut the cap off the pen. Be careful not to cut into the ink barrel. *Caution:* Aim the pen away from yourself and others!

5. Pull the rose off its stem. Notice the small remaining stem underneath the rose.

6. Insert the remaining stem into the top of the pen, and glue it in place.

7. Keeping it taut, wrap the floral tape down the pen, starting just beneath the rose, until you get to the metal writing tip. Tear off excess tape.

8. Insert your flower pen into the Styrofoam® hole, far enough to hold it upright. Be careful not to bunch up the tape.

9. Place the moss inside the clay pot, covering the Styrofoam® ball.

10. Tie the red ribbon into a bow underneath the flower.

The fountain pen was invented in 1883.

VALENTINE BLACKBOARD (K-3)

SUPPLIES

Red paint marker (fine)	Red curling ribbon
Blackboard set (party favor set)	Scissors
	Wrapped Valentine sucker

DIRECTIONS

1. Use the paint marker to decorate the outer rim of the blackboard with hearts. Write "Happy Valentine's Day" at the top edge and let dry (approximately 5 to 10 minutes).

2. Lay the chalk and sponge eraser, which comes with the blackboard set, in the center of the blackboard. Wrap the ribbon around the board going both directions, tie tightly, and curl the ends with the scissors.

3. Slide the sucker between the ribbon and chalk.

Note: Older children have said they would like this favor. Use your judgement.

VALENTINE SODA FOUNTAIN DECORATION (K-6)

SUPPLIES

Soda fountain glass (found at craft stores)

Red cinnamon candy

3-inch round Styrofoam® ball

Glue gun

Flexible plastic straw

Peppermint candy

Straight pins

This makes a great gift - perhaps for the teacher.

DIRECTIONS

1. Wash and dry the glass.
2. Pour the cinnamon candy into the glass, almost filling it to the top.
3. Push the Styrofoam® ball snugly into the glass. (Spill-out some cinnamon candies if needed.) Glue the ball in place, or it will shift when adding candy.
4. Poke the straw through the Styrofoam® ball at any angle.
5. Attach the peppermint candies to the ball with straight pins, starting from the bottom at the edge of the glass, working your way up towards the top. To hold the candy firmly to the Styrofoam® ball, stick the straight pins into the twisted part of the wrappers.
6. Continue to attach the candy until the ball is completely covered.

Note: Younger children may need help with the straight pins.

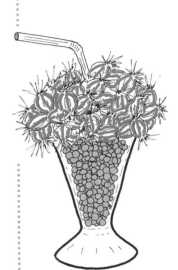

BUTTON BRACELET (K-3)

SUPPLIES

Red pipe cleaner

Four two-holed heart-buttons

DIRECTIONS

1. Measure the child's wrist. Cut the pipe cleaner to match the length of the child's wrist, but add 2 inches.
2. Push the pipe cleaner through one hole of a button, leaving 1 inch of the pipe cleaner past the hole. Then thread the long end of the pipe cleaner through the other hole of the same button, pulling it tight.
3. Insert the pipe cleaner up through another button the same way, with the heart tip pointing the same direction as the first button. Keep enough pipe cleaner between the buttons so they don't overlap.
4. Continue to attach buttons as in Step #2, until 1 inch of the pipe cleaner remains.
5. Wrap the bracelet around the child's wrist and twist the ends together to secure.

99

SUPPLIES FOR FEBRUARY & PRESIDENTS' CRAFTS & FAVORS

SWEET SMELLING CHERRY PIE (K-6)

- Potpourri (cherry scent)
- 9-inch disposable pie pan
- 9 x 9-inch light brown cotton fabric
- Zigzag scissors
- Glue gun

LOG CABIN KIT (K-6)

- Pretzel rods
- Bread knife
- Canned chocolate frosting
- Butter knife
- 5-inch square heavy mat board (neutral color)
- 5 x 8-inch brown poster board
- Rectangular butter cookie
- Heart-shaped candy

VALENTINE ROSE PEN (K-6)

- Egg-shaped Styrofoam® ball
- Knife
- Small clay pot
- Bic® pen (any color)
- Scissors
- Artificial rose
- Glue gun
- 25 inches green floral tape
- Craft moss
- 6 inches ⅛" red ribbon

VALENTINE BLACKBOARD (K-3)

- Red paint marker (fine)
- Blackboard set (party favor set)
- Red curling ribbon
- Scissors
- Wrapped Valentine sucker

VALENTINE SODA FOUNTAIN DECORATION (K-6)

- Soda fountain glass (found at craft stores)
- Red cinnamon candy
- 3-inch round Styrofoam® ball
- Glue gun
- Flexible plastic straw
- Peppermint candy
- Straight pins

BUTTON BRACELET (K-3)

- Red pipe cleaner
- Four two-holed heart-buttons

Don't forget the camera and film.

ALL-TIME FAVORITE CRAFTS & FAVORS

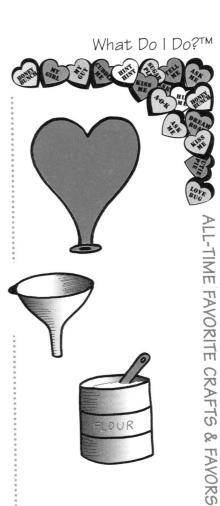

SMOOSHIES (K-6)

SUPPLIES

Heavy heart-shaped balloon (found at party stores)

Funnel

1 cup flour

DIRECTIONS

1. Stretch the balloon for a few minutes before filling.

2. Using the funnel, fill the balloon with 1 cup of flour. Depending on the size of the balloon you may need to add more flour. To get the flour as far down inside the balloon as possible, gently tap the balloon as you fill it.

3. Remove as much air as possible and tie the end of the balloon.

Note: Do not use balloons sold in packages for birthday parties. They are too thin and can break.

VALENTINE TIC-TAC-TOE (K-6)

SUPPLIES

9 x 12-inch red felt

Pencil

Scissors

Red thread

Needle

20 inches white rickrack

Tacky glue or fabric glue

White felt

Optional: White pipe cleaners

#1

#2

DIRECTIONS

1. Fold the red felt in half to measure 9 x 6-inches.

2. Trace a heart shape onto the red felt. Cut it out to make two felt hearts.

3. Thread the needle, knot, and sew the two hearts together around the edges, leaving an opening at the top to store the X's and O's. You may prefer to use fabric glue to attach the two hearts together.

4. Cut the rickrack into four equal pieces. Glue it on one side of the heart to form a Tic-Tac-Toe grid, two pieces one way and two pieces the other.

5. Trace the following pattern pieces onto the white felt and cut out: five "X's" (pattern piece #1) and five "O's" (pattern piece #2).

6. Put the X's and O's inside the heart.

7. To play Valentine Tic-Tac-Toe, follow the directions for Human Valentine Tic-Tac-Toe on Page 55.

Optional: Use white pipe cleaners instead of white felt to form the X's and O's.

ALL-TIME FAVORITE CRAFTS & FAVORS

CANDY-FILLED GLASS (K-6)

SUPPLIES

15 inches red cellophane wrap

Valentine candy

Plastic margarita glass

12 inches red curling ribbon (wide with wire edge)

DIRECTIONS

1. Lay the cellophane flat on a table.
2. Put candy into the margarita glass and pour that amount, plus enough to overfill the glass, onto the cellophane wrap.
3. Gather up the edges of the wrap and tie with the ribbon.
4. Put the bag of candy into the margarita glass.

Note: Any clear plastic glass will work. A margarita glass has a little more pizzazz, but may be more expensive.

TOOTH FAIRY VALENTINE PILLOW (K-1)

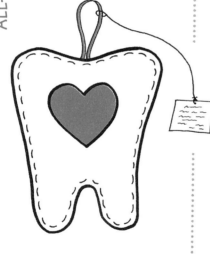

SUPPLIES

Pencil

7-inch square white felt

3-inch square red felt

Scissors

Red thread

Sewing machine

Straight pins

White thread

Polyester stuffing

10 inches 1/8" red ribbon

Red permanent marker

1 1/2-inch square white cardstock

Paper hole puncher

10 inches red embroidery floss with needle

February is National Children's Dental Health Month.
Special Thanks to Paula Farney for sharing her pillow idea.

DIRECTIONS

1. Trace the following pattern pieces onto the felt and cut out: two white teeth (pattern piece #1) and one red heart (pattern piece #2).
2. Thread the sewing machine with red thread and sew the red heart to one tooth.
3. Pin the white felt pieces together, making sure the red heart is on top.
4. Re-thread your machine with white thread and sew the tooth edges together, leaving the top of the tooth open enough to stuff it. You do not need to turn the tooth inside out.
5. Fill the tooth with the stuffing.
6. Fold the ribbon in half, then insert the ends into the top of the tooth, and sew the tooth pillow closed. (Take out excess stuffing if needed.)
7. Write the following saying on the cardstock:

> Put your tooth
> In this wee place
> And put a smile
> On the Tooth Fairy's face.

8. Punch a hole in the paper, lace the floss through it, and tie to secure. Tie the other end to the ribbon, and slide paper into the heart.

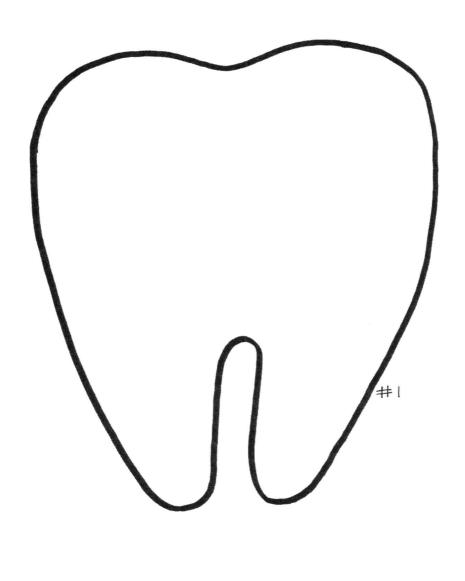

#1

#2

CORRUGATED STAMP CRAFT (K-6)

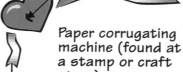

SUPPLIES

Paper corrugating machine (found at a stamp or craft store)

3 x 4-inch white poster board

Glue gun

3½ x 4½-inch mat board (any color)

7 inches wire (19 gauge)

Packing tape

Cartoon character stamp

Stamp with Valentine message

Black ink pad

Permanent markers (assorted colors)

DIRECTIONS

1. Corrugate the white poster board, then glue onto the mat board, leaving a ½-inch margin

2. Curve the wire into an arc and tape the ends onto the back of the mat board.

3. Stamp the cartoon character onto the corrugated board, and then stamp the Valentine message next to the character.

4. Color in the character with the permanent markers.

5. Write "Happy Valentine's Day," the child's name, and the year on the mat board.

Note: You may be able to find corrugated paper at the craft store instead of using the machine.

Did you know that there used to be a book filled with verses called *The Valentine Writer?* Easy to use, people decided on verses that they liked and copied them onto cards to give on Valentine's Day.

VALENTINE CARD JOURNAL (K-1)

SUPPLIES

Thirty-two pieces 9 x 12-inch white construction paper

Crayons

Copy of Valentine chart on page 105

Paper hole puncher

Two 6-inch pieces red yarn

Rubber cement

A special keepsake to hold Valentines for years to come!

DIRECTIONS

1. Have each child draw a picture with crayons on one piece of white construction paper. Ask them to draw what "Valentines" mean to them.

2. Stack all of the construction paper together by placing the child's drawing on top followed by the Valentine chart, and then the remaining paper.

3. Punch two holes into the construction paper (a few pieces at a time) about ½ inch from the edge. Either side will work depending on the drawing.

4. Thread one piece of yarn through each hole and tie in bows to hold the journal together.

5. Glue the Valentine cards you wish to save on the blank pages.

Note: For older children grades 2 to 6, refer to "Valentine Diary" in Post Office Crafts & Favors section.

VALENTINE CHART

1. Fill in each child's name that gives you a Valentine card, their grade, teacher's name, and a description of each Valentine.

2. Put this journal in a safe place so you can enjoy it when you are older. You may wish to show it to your children or grandchildren one day.

Name	Grade/Year	Teacher	Description

ALL-TIME FAVORITE CRAFTS & FAVORS

SILHOUETTE FOR MOM & DAD (K-6)

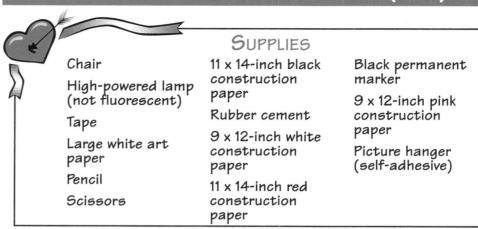

SUPPLIES

Chair

High-powered lamp (not fluorescent)

Tape

Large white art paper

Pencil

Scissors

11 x 14-inch black construction paper

Rubber cement

9 x 12-inch white construction paper

11 x 14-inch red construction paper

Black permanent marker

9 x 12-inch pink construction paper

Picture hanger (self-adhesive)

DIRECTIONS

1. Place a chair sideways about 6 inches from the bare wall.

2. Have the child sit in the chair.

3. Aim the light at the child's head and the wall. His shadow will then appear on the wall.

4. Adjust the distance and angle of the light from the wall until you get the best shadow.

5. Tape the white art paper onto the wall where the child's shadow falls, centering the shadow on the paper. Only the shadow from the child's head should appear on the paper. If needed, adjust the chair closer or farther away from the wall.

6. Ask the child to hold very still while you trace his shadow onto the paper with the pencil. After you capture his silhouette, he may get off the chair.

7. Cut out the child's silhouette using the scissors, and then trace it onto the black construction paper. Cut out the black silhouette.

8. Glue the black silhouette onto the white construction paper.

9. Glue the white construction paper onto the 11 x 14-inch red construction paper.

10. Use the black permanent marker to draw a line between the white and red construction paper.

11. Cut four 3-inch hearts from the 9 x 12-inch pink construction paper.

12. Glue these hearts to the silhouette's "frame," one on each corner, tips pointing toward the center of the picture.

13. Attach the picture hanger to the back of the silhouette.

SUPPLIES FOR ALL-TIME FAVORITE CRAFTS & FAVORS

SMOOSHIES (K-6)

Heavy heart-shaped balloon (found at party stores)

Funnel

1 cup flour

VALENTINE TIC-TAC-TOE (K-6)

9 x 12-inch red felt

Pencil

Scissors

Red thread

Needle

20 inches white rickrack

Tacky glue or fabric glue

White felt

Optional: White pipe cleaners

CANDY-FILLED GLASS (K-6)

15 inches red cellophane wrap

Valentine candy

Plastic margarita glass

12 inches red curling ribbon (wide with wire edge)

TOOTH FAIRY VALENTINE PILLOW (K-1)

Pencil

7-inch square white felt

3-inch square red felt

Scissors

Red thread

Sewing machine

Straight pins

White thread

Polyester stuffing

10 inches 1/8" red ribbon

Red permanent marker

1 1/2 inch square white cardstock

Paper hole puncher

10 inches red embroidery floss with needle

CORRUGATED STAMP CRAFT (K-6)

Paper corrugating machine (found at a stamp or craft store)

3 x 4-inch white poster board

Glue gun

3 1/2 x 4 1/2-inch mat board (any color)

7 inches wire (19 gauge)

Packing tape

Cartoon character stamp

Stamp with Valentine message

Black ink pad

Permanent markers (assorted colors)

VALENTINE CARD JOURNAL (K-1)

Thirty-two pieces 9 x 12-inch white construction paper

Crayons

Copy of Valentine chart

Paper hole puncher

Two 6-inch pieces red yarn

Rubber cement

SILHOUETTE FOR MOM & DAD (K-6)

Chair

High-powered lamp (not fluorescent)

Large white art paper

Tape

Pencil

Scissors

11 x 14-inch black construction paper

Rubber cement

9 x 12-inch white construction paper

11 x 14-inch red construction paper

Black permanent marker

9 x 12-inch pink construction paper

Picture hanger (self-adhesive)

CHAPTER FOUR
SWEETS

HELPFUL HINTS FOR SWEETS

1. Remember to check with the teacher for any children with braces or food allergies.

2. It is best to serve two different sweets, so you're sure to please everyone.

3. *Always, always* have extra sweets for the teacher, parent helpers, and siblings. Give janitors any leftover sweets. They really appreciate it.

4. Always read the recipes to see if there are steps to do ahead of time or waiting periods.

5. Sweets can sometimes take longer than planned. Prepare as much of the recipe as possible days before the party.

6. Be sure you have all the ingredients and supplies before beginning any recipe.

7. Some recipes, such as Caterpillar Gum and Gumdrop Teddy Bear, may look difficult to make but are very easy. Give them a try!

8. Have children bring stuffed animals or dolls to the Valentine party. Bake or buy miniature cookies so the children can pretend to feed them.

9. For easy Valentine sweets, wrap store-bought cookies in plastic wrap, secure with red curling ribbon and attach a note card saying "Happy Valentine's Day."

10. To make heart-shaped cupcakes, place a marble between the filled cupcake liner and the cupcake pan before baking.

11. Use Valentine cookie cutters to cut out waffles or bread to make sandwiches.

12. When adding peanut butter or shortening to measuring cups, first rinse with water. The moisture helps the sticky mixture slide out easier.

13. Baker's Joy® is an oil and flour spray used for baking. Much easier than oiling and flouring bakeware.

14. A double boiler is a combination of two saucepans fitting together, one inside the other. Water is placed in the bottom saucepan and the ingredients are placed in the top saucepan. When the water boils, it cooks or melts the ingredients in the top saucepan. Or use a glass bowl in the microwave, but be sure to check often and stir.

15. A Valentine jelly heart is also a gummy heart and can be plain with or without sugar, or cinnamon-flavored with or without sugar.

HEART SWEETS

HEART TOAST (K-6)

INGREDIENTS AND SUPPLIES

Toaster	Butter
Bread	Strawberry spread
Heart-shaped cookie cutter	Cinnamon sugar
Two butter knives	*Makes one toast*

Perfect for those morning parties!

Caution: Always have a parent assist when using the toaster.

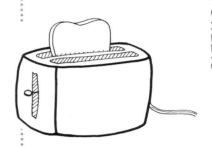

DIRECTIONS

1. Each child toasts his own bread, and then cuts it with the heart-shaped cookie cutter.

2. The child then chooses to spread butter or strawberry spread on the heart toast. Cinnamon sugar sprinkled on top of the buttered toast is also a favorite!

HEART-SHAPED PIZZAS (K-6)

INGREDIENTS AND SUPPLIES

Toothpicks (one per child)	Serving bowls
Assorted permanent markers	Serving spoons
Pizza dough (homemade or store-bought kit)	Several baking sheets
	Napkins
Pizza sauce	*Optional:* Pizza toppings
Mozzarella cheese	*Modify this recipe to serve the entire class*
Pepperoni	

DIRECTIONS

1. Color the tips of toothpicks using permanent markers. These will be used to color code the children's pizzas.

2. Form the dough into heart shapes.

3. Place the ingredients into the bowls with the spoons. Let the children create their own pizzas. Then have each child stick his toothpick in his pizza, colored tip up.

4. Place the pizzas on the baking sheets, with no more than one of each colored toothpick per sheet. Give each baking sheet a number. Have the children remember which color they picked and which baking sheet number it's on. This way the children are sure to get their own pizzas.

5. Bake at 400° in the school's kitchen oven until the dough is brown and the cheese has melted.

6. Cool slightly and serve on napkins.

Note: Get permission to use the school's kitchen.

Optional: A few days before the party, take a vote with the class on their favorite pizza toppings.

Variation: Form the dough into heart shapes and pre-bake them before the party begins. Then let the children create their own pizzas. Broil pizzas in the oven until hot or the cheese has melted.

111

HEART SWEETS

MAKE & BAKE PUZZLE COOKIES (K-6)

INGREDIENTS AND SUPPLIES

- Wilton® mini heart pan
- Baker's Joy®
- Favorite cookie recipe
- Cutting board
- Two decorating bags
- Decorating tips #4 and #5
- Two decorating couplers
- 16-ounce can red frosting
- 16-ounce can white frosting
- Sharp knife
- Red plates (one per puzzle cookie)

Makes approximately 5 to 6 cookies

DIRECTIONS

1. Spray the pan with Baker's Joy® following the directions on the can.

2. Make and bake your favorite cookie recipe. (A lot of kids like chocolate chip!) Bake one cookie at a time using the heart pan, and let it cool in the pan.

3. Turn the cookie out onto your hand, then flip it onto the cutting board. Wash and dry the pan before baking each cookie.

4. Fill one bag with red frosting, and the other bag with white frosting. Attach a tip to each.

5. Use a sharp knife to cut each heart into a puzzle. Push the puzzle back in place to decorate with a Valentine saying and design, using both colors of frosting. Let the frosting dry.

6. Separate the puzzle pieces and serve scattered on a plate, retaining a resemblance of a heart.

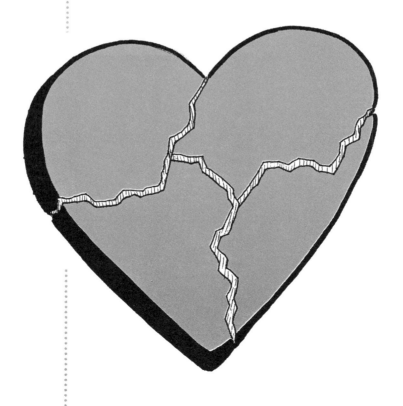

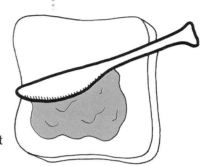

MINI ROLLED-UP HEARTS (K-6)

INGREDIENTS AND SUPPLIES

Butter knife

Red jelly

One slice bread

Sharp knife

This recipe makes 5 mini hearts

Cute and Easy!

DIRECTIONS

1. Spread jelly onto the bread.
2. Trim the crust off the bread.
3. Roll the bread up, jellyroll style.
4. Slice the roll into five sections, each about $1/2$ inch wide.
5. Lay the sections flat and use your fingers to form them into heart shapes.

SWEETHEART (K-6)

INGREDIENTS AND SUPPLIES

Two wrapped candy canes

Glue gun

Two conversation candy hearts

6 inches red ribbon

Makes one heart

DIRECTIONS

1. Keep the candy canes wrapped and put them together to form a heart. Glue at the top and bottom of the heart where the candy canes cross.

2. Glue the conversation hearts where the candy canes are joined together.

3. Make a loop with the ribbon and glue behind the top of the heart for a hanger.

113

INGREDIENTS AND SUPPLIES FOR HEART SWEETS

HEART TOAST (K-6)

- Toaster
- Bread
- Heart-shaped cookie cutter
- Two butter knives
- Butter
- Strawberry spread
- Cinnamon sugar

HEART-SHAPED PIZZAS (K-6)

- Toothpicks (one per child)
- Assorted permanent markers
- Pizza dough (homemade or store-bought kit)
- Pizza sauce
- Mozzarella cheese
- Pepperoni
- Serving bowls
- Serving spoons
- Several baking sheets
- Napkins
- *Optional: Pizza toppings*

MAKE & BAKE PUZZLE COOKIES (K-6)

- Wilton® mini heart pan
- Baker's Joy®
- Favorite cookie recipe
- Cutting board
- Two decorating bags
- Decorating tips, #4 and #5
- Two decorating couplers
- 16-ounce can red frosting
- 16-ounce can white frosting
- Sharp knife
- Red plates (one per puzzle cookie)

MINI ROLLED UP HEARTS (K-6)

- Butter Knife
- Red jelly
- One slice bread
- Sharp knife

SWEETHEART (K-6)

- Two wrapped candy canes
- Glue gun
- Two conversation candy hearts
- 6 inches red ribbon

Don't forget the camera and film.

CUPID SWEETS

CHEWY HEART ARROW (K-6)

INGREDIENTS AND SUPPLIES
4-inch wooden skewer

Three Valentine jelly hearts

Makes one arrow

DIRECTIONS

1. Slide the pointed end of the skewer into the first heart.

2. Slide the second and third heart onto the skewer, pointing them the same direction. Push all the hearts together so they touch. The remainder of the skewer will be used to pick the arrow up.

MARSHMALLOW BOW & ARROW (K-6)

INGREDIENTS AND SUPPLIES

Six to seven marshmallow hearts

10-inch wooden skewer

Valentine jelly heart

Scissors

1 x 2-inch red construction paper

Makes one arrow

DIRECTIONS

1. Slide the marshmallow hearts horizontally onto the pointed end of the skewer. Leave approximately 1½ inches of the non-pointed end exposed.

2. Slide the jelly heart vertically onto the pointed end of the skewer, so its tip points the same direction as the skewer.

3. Using the scissors, fringe the paper lengthwise staying ½ inch from the end.

4. Roll up the paper widthwise to form the arrow feathers and push it into the last marshmallow heart to secure.

115

CUPID SWEETS

CHEESE & PRETZEL ARROWS (K-6)

INGREDIENTS AND SUPPLIES

Knife

1-inch cube cheddar cheese

Two pretzel sticks

Two 1-inch slices Twizzlers®
Cherry Pull-n-Peel™ candy

Makes 2 arrows

DIRECTIONS

1. Using the knife, cut the cheese cube diagonally, making two arrow points.
2. Slide one piece of cheese onto one end of a pretzel stick to form the point of an arrow. Save the other piece for another arrow.
3. On the opposite end of the pretzel stick, carefully push on a piece of licorice.
4. Slightly peel the licorice apart to form arrow feathers.
5. Repeat steps 2 to 4 to make the second arrow.

QUICK & EASY DONUT ARROW (K-6)

INGREDIENTS AND SUPPLIES

4-inch wooden skewer

1-inch Valentine jelly heart

Two powdered bite-sized donuts

Scissors

1 x 2-inch red craft foam (found at craft stores)

Makes one arrow

DIRECTIONS

1. Slide the pointed end of the skewer into the top of the jelly heart so its tip side is pointing out.
2. Then slide the two donuts onto the skewer from the other end of the skewer.
3. Using the scissors, fringe the foam lengthwise, staying ½ inch from the end.
4. Roll up the foam widthwise. Slide it onto the open end of the skewer and into the hole of the donuts to secure it.

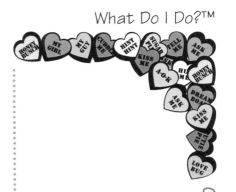

CUPID'S EASY TARGET HEART (K-6)

INGREDIENTS AND SUPPLIES

Decorating gel (any color)

Heart-shaped snack cake (found in grocery stores around Valentine's Day)

Cellophane frills toothpick

Makes one target

DIRECTIONS

1. Using the decorating gel, draw a large heart on the top of the snack cake.

2. Draw another heart inside the first heart and so on until you have a small enough heart for a "bull's eye."

3. Place the toothpick into the center of the smallest heart, hitting the "bull's eye."

CHOCOLATE-DIPPED STRAWBERRIES (K-6)

INGREDIENTS AND SUPPLIES

24 to 30 large strawberries

12-ounce bag semi-sweet chocolate chips

Double boiler pan or microwave bowl

24 to 30 Valentine cupcake liners

Makes 24 to 30 strawberries

Cupid's favorite!

DIRECTIONS

1. Wash and dry the strawberries, keeping the stems on.

2. Melt the chocolate chips in a double boiler pan, or in a microwave.

3. Dip the tips of each strawberry into the melted chocolate, covering about ¾ of the strawberry. Shake off any excess chocolate and lay each strawberry into its own cupcake liner.

INGREDIENTS AND SUPPLIES FOR CUPID SWEETS

CHEWY HEART ARROW (K-6)

4-inch wooden skewer

Three Valentine jelly hearts

MARSHMALLOW BOW & ARROW (K-6)

Six to seven marshmallow hearts

10-inch wooden skewer

Valentine jelly heart

Scissors

1 x 2-inch red construction paper

CHEESE & PRETZEL ARROWS (K-6)

Knife

1-inch cube cheddar cheese

Two pretzel sticks

Two 1-inch slices Twizzlers® Cherry Pull-n-Peel™ candy

QUICK & EASY DONUT ARROW (K-6)

4-inch wooden skewer

1-inch Valentine jelly heart

Two powdered bite-sized donuts

Scissors

1 x 2-inch red craft foam (found at craft stores)

CUPID'S EASY TARGET HEART (K-6)

Decorating gel (any color)

Heart-shaped snack cake (found in grocery stores around Valentine's Day)

Cellophane frills toothpick

CHOCOLATE-DIPPED STRAWBERRIES (K-6)

24 to 30 large strawberries

12-ounce bag semi-sweet chocolate chips

Double boiler pan or microwave bowl

24 to 30 Valentine cupcake liners

Don't forget the camera and film.

LOVE & FRIENDSHIP SWEETS

FUNNEL KISS (K-6)

INGREDIENTS AND SUPPLIES

Butter or margarine

Large or small funnel

Kellogg's™ Rice Krispies® Cereal

Marshmallows

Measuring cups

Large saucepan

Spoon or spatula

Clear wrap

Aluminum foil

Short narrow strips of paper

Red permanent marker

Makes 6 large kisses or 12 small kisses

DIRECTIONS

1. Butter the inside of the funnel and set aside.
2. Make a batch of Rice Krispies Treats® using the recipe on the cereal box.
3. While warm, press the mixture into the funnel, forming a kiss.
4. Slide the kiss out of the funnel onto a piece of clear wrap big enough to cover it.
5. Wrap the kiss (to prevent sticking), then wrap again with aluminum foil around the bottom and up to the top.
6. On the strip of paper write "Happy Valentine's Day!"
7. Slide the strip of paper between the foil and the kiss top before sealing the foil completely.
8. Continue making kisses, keeping the funnel buttered. Re-warm the mixture as necessary (a microwave works great for this!)

"For extra fun and flavor, sprinkle 1½ ounces of powdered red gelatin dessert into the melted butter and marshmallow mixture. Mix well before adding the cereal. To add a special touch, use a computer to print "Heartfelt" messages on strips of paper and insert between the foil and kiss top."

Becky Leon
Littleton, Colorado

COOKIE BOUQUET (K-6)

INGREDIENTS AND SUPPLIES

Styrofoam®

6-inch clean terra cotta flowerpot

Two dozen wooden skewers

Four dozen Valentine jelly hearts

Two dozen flower-shaped cookies with holes in the center

Scissors

4 yards 4⅛" red ribbon

2 to 3 cups popped popcorn

Makes 2 dozen cookie flowers

DIRECTIONS

1. Push the Styrofoam® into the bottom of the flowerpot.
2. Make a cookie flower by pushing the sharp end of a skewer into the tip of a jelly heart. From the dull end of the skewer, slide a cookie onto the skewer and then another jelly heart (tip toward the cookie). Keep the flower at the sharp end of the skewer.
3. Cut the ribbon into two dozen 6-inch pieces. Tie one piece into a bow onto the skewer, beneath the heart under the cookie flower.
4. Continue making cookie flowers until you have two dozen.
5. Trim the skewer sticks so you have assorted heights of flowers.
6. Arrange the cookie skewers into the Styrofoam®.
7. Add the popped popcorn to hide the Styrofoam®.

A love knot, meaning endless love, consists of intertwined loops, with no beginning or end. People would write messages on the loops and give them to their special someone.

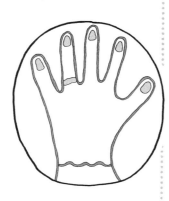

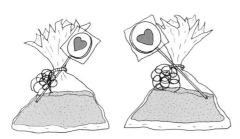

LOVER'S KNOTS (K-6)

INGREDIENTS AND SUPPLIES

7 ounces Wilton® White Candy Melts™

Medium saucepan or microwave bowl

Spoon or spatula

10 ounces Decorating Decors red-sugar crystals

Plate

10-ounce bag pretzel twists

Wax paper

Makes about 60 knots

DIRECTIONS

1. Melt the Candy Melts™ over low heat in the saucepan, stirring constantly, or in a microwave.
2. Empty the red sugar onto the plate.
3. Grasp the pretzel at the X and dip it into the candy, only covering one side. Work quickly. Shake slightly to let any excess candy drop off into the saucepan.
4. Immediately dip the coated side of the pretzel into the red-colored sugar to coat.
5. Lay the pretzel, sugar side up, on the wax paper to harden for at least one hour.
6. Continue making the Lover's Knots until you have the desired amount.

COOKIE HANDS (K-6)

INGREDIENTS AND SUPPLIES

Roll of refrigerated sugar cookie dough

Assorted decorating gels   Makes approximately 6 cookies

DIRECTIONS

1. Prior to the party, make and bake 6-inch round cookies.
2. Give each child one cookie. Have the children place their hands on their cookies, and trace them with decorating gel.
3. The children can then use the gels to decorate their cookie hands with nails, rings, bracelets, etc.

FRIENDSHIP POWDER (K-6)

INGREDIENTS AND SUPPLIES

Two 3-ounce packages gelatin dessert (any flavor)

Two small sandwich bags

Two Valentine suckers

Two 6-inch pieces red curling ribbon

Two 6-inch pieces white curling ribbon

Scissors

Makes enough for one child and one friend.

DIRECTIONS

1. Pour each package of gelatin into its own sandwich bag.
2. Tie a sucker onto each bag with one piece of red ribbon and one piece of white ribbon. Curl the ribbon with the scissors.
3. If desired, trim any excess plastic off the top of each bag.
4. Give the two bags of Friendship Powder to a child. He keeps one and gives the other to a friend. Encourage him to find a friend who hasn't been given any friendship powder!

INGREDIENTS AND SUPPLIES FOR LOVE & FRIENDSHIP SWEETS

FUNNEL KISS (K-6)

- Butter or margarine
- Large or small funnel
- Kellogg's™ Rice Krispies® Cereal
- Marshmallows
- Measuring cups
- Large saucepan
- Spoon or spatula
- Clear wrap
- Aluminum foil
- Short narrow strips of paper
- Red permanent marker

COOKIE BOUQUET (K-6)

- Styrofoam®
- 6-inch clean terra cotta flowerpot
- Two dozen wooden skewers
- Four dozen Valentine jelly hearts
- Two dozen flower-shaped cookies with holes in the center
- Scissors
- 4 yards 1/8" red ribbon
- 2 to 3 cups popped popcorn

LOVER'S KNOTS (K-6)

- 7 ounces Wilton® White Candy Melts™
- Medium saucepan or microwave bowl
- Spoon or spatula
- 10 ounces Decorating Decors red-sugar crystals
- Plate
- 10 ounce bag pretzel twists
- Wax paper

COOKIE HANDS (K-6)

- Roll of refrigerated sugar cookie dough
- Assorted decorating gels

FRIENDSHIP POWDER (K-6)

- Two 3-ounce packages gelatin dessert (any flavor)
- Two small sandwich bags
- Two Valentine suckers
- Two 6-inch pieces red curling ribbon
- Two 6-inch pieces white curling ribbon
- Scissors

Don't forget the camera and film.

ANIMAL SWEETS

DOGGIE ROLL (K-6)

INGREDIENTS AND SUPPLIES

Five Hershey's Kisses® (red)

Smarties® candy roll

Glue gun

Two 7 mm moving eyes

1-inch square red felt

Scissors

5 mm black pom-pom

1-inch piece pipe cleaner (any color)

Makes one dog

Hershey's Kisses®, first made in 1907 and celebrating their 90th anniversary, are produced today at a rate of 80 millon per day.

DIRECTIONS

1. At one end of the candy roll, glue a kiss on each side, flat part down. At the other end of the roll, glue two more kisses, one on each side with flat parts down. Now the dog has legs and paws.
2. Glue the flat part of the fifth kiss to one end of the candy roll to make the head.
3. Glue the moving eyes to the top portion of the head (kiss).
4. Cut two floppy ears out of the red felt and glue to the head behind the eyes.
5. Glue the pom-pom to the tip of the head for the nose.
6. Glue the piece of pipe cleaner to the other end of the candy roll for the dog's tail.

EASY DINOSAUR ICE CREAM SANDWICH (K-6)

INGREDIENTS AND SUPPLIES

½ cup ice cream (any flavor)

Butter knife

Two dinosaur graham crackers

Makes one sandwich

DIRECTIONS

1. Soften the ice cream until it's easy to spread.
2. Spread the ice cream onto the flat side of one graham cracker.
3. Carefully press the flat side of the second graham cracker onto the ice cream side of the first cracker.
4. Put the ice cream sandwich into the freezer until hard, approximately two hours.

GUMDROP TEDDY BEAR (K-6)

INGREDIENTS AND SUPPLIES

Knife	Two small green gumdrops
Large red gumdrop	Two small yellow gumdrops
Two red M&M's®	Small heart-shaped candy
Meringue (ingredients and recipe below)	Lollipop stick
Decorating bag	Styrofoam® (used as a drying base)
Decorating coupler	*Optional:* A sandwich bag and Valentine ribbon
Decorating tip, #4 or #5	
Large green gumdrop	*Makes one teddy bear*

MERINGUE:

Wilton® Meringue powder mix	Mixer and bowl
Powdered sugar	Spoon or spatula
Water	

DIRECTIONS

1. With the knife, slit two opposite sides of the red gumdrop (head), big enough to slide in M&Ms® for the bear's ears.

2. Follow the directions on the can of meringue powder to make a recipe of royal icing.

3. Working quickly, put the royal icing into the decorating bag, coupler and tip already in place.

4. Squeeze the icing on top of the large green gumdrop (body), then quickly attach the bottom of the red gumdrop (head).

5. Again, working quickly, attach the small green gumdrops (arms), one on each side of the large green gumdrop.

6. Quickly attach the bottoms of the two yellow gumdrops (legs), to the bottom of the large green gumdrop.

7. Attach a heart-shaped candy to the center of the bear's body.

8. Push the lollipop stick into the bottom of the green gumdrop, and stick it into the Styrofoam® for a few hours to let the bear harden. Take it out of the Styrofoam® before serving. This is an edible bear.

9. Draw eyes and a mouth on the head using the royal icing.

Optional: Slide the hardened Gumdrop Teddy Bear into a baggie and tie with Valentine ribbon.

What does Valentine's Day mean to you?

"Candy and happy."
Rob Taylor, Age 8

"Love" and "Valentines."
Travis and Kaylyn Cooper
Ages 6 and 4

ANIMAL SWEETS

SWEET ANIMAL COOKIES (K-6)

INGREDIENTS AND SUPPLIES

Six animal cookies (3 pairs of matching cookies)

3 teaspoons pink or red canned frosting

Butter knife

Makes 3 cookies

Sweet!

DIRECTIONS

1. Spread one teaspoon frosting onto the flat side of an animal cookie from each pair. You will now have three frosted cookies.

2. Using the same "animals," place their flat sides onto the frosting sides of the first cookies, matching the edges of the cookies.

The King Cobra is a very poisonous snake, its venom can kill an adult elephant.

SNAKE BITES (K-6)

INGREDIENTS AND SUPPLIES

Scissors

42 inches white curling ribbon

3 feet red plastic wrap

Six individual bags of Valentine candy

3-inch square green construction paper

¼ x 2-inch red construction paper

Tacky glue

Black permanent marker

Makes one snake

Very, very cute!

DIRECTIONS

1. Cut the curling ribbon into seven 6-inch sections.

2. Carefully lay the plastic wrap on a table.

3. Lay the candy down the center of the plastic wrap, leaving a 2-inch space between each candy and a 3-inch space at each end.

4. Roll the long sides of the plastic wrap around the candy, being careful not to let the candy shift.

5. Tie pieces of ribbon between the bags of candy and at each end. Curl the ribbons with the scissors.

6. Cut a heart-shaped head from the green construction paper.

7. Cut out a snake tongue from the red construction paper and glue under the snake's head at the heart's tip.

8. With the black permanent marker, draw two hearts for eyes, with solid hearts for the pupils, and two short vertical lines for the nose.

9. Glue the head to one end of the snake's body.

PUPPY TREATS (K-6)

INGREDIENTS AND SUPPLIES

½ cup butter (one stick)

½ cup peanut butter

6-ounce bag semi-sweet chocolate chips

Medium saucepan or microwave bowl

Spoon or spatula

1 cup Cheerios®

9 cups rice cereal squares

Large bowl

2 cups powdered sugar

Ten small sandwich bags

Ten 5-inch pieces black curling ribbon

Ten 5-inch pieces red curling ribbon

Ten blank note cards

Scissors

Black permanent marker

Paper hole puncher

Optional: New, clean dog bowl and scoop

Makes 10 treats

DIRECTIONS

1. Melt the butter, peanut butter, and chocolate chips in the saucepan over low heat, or in a microwave, stirring constantly.

2. Mix both cereals together in the large bowl.

3. Pour the melted mixture over the cereal, mix well.

4. Sprinkle the powdered sugar over the cereal mixture and mix until the cereal is coated.

5. Pour one cup of Puppy Treats into each sandwich bag. Tie each bag with one piece of red ribbon, and one piece of black ribbon.

6. Draw the dog paw print (below) on each note card and cut out. Color in the paws with the black permanent marker. Punch a hole into each card.

7. Thread each bag's ribbons through the hole of the dog paw note card, and tie close to the bag. Curl any excess ribbon with the scissors.

Variation: Instead of making individual bags of Puppy Treats, place the Puppy Treats in a new, clean dog bowl and let the children scoop out their own serving.

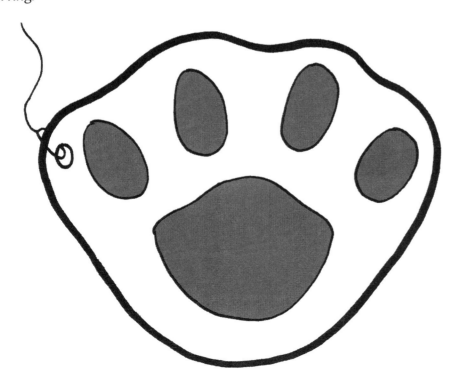

ANIMAL SWEETS

ANIMAL SWEETS

CATERPILLAR GUM (K-6)

INGREDIENTS AND SUPPLIES

1½ x 4½-inch cardboard	Wilton® Yellow Icing Color
2 x 5-inch red foil	Three spoons
Tape	Three kitchen towels
Meringue (ingredients and recipe below)	Three decorating bags
	Three decorating couplers
Three small bowls	Decorating tips, #2, #3, #5, and #12
Three toothpicks	
Wilton® Black Icing Color	Seven small green gumballs
Wilton® Green Icing Color	

MERINGUE:	Mixer and bowl
Wilton® Meringue Powder Mix	Spoon or spatula
Powdered sugar	
Water	Makes one caterpillar

DIRECTIONS

1. Wrap the cardboard with red foil. Tape if needed under the bottom.

2. Follow the directions on the can of the meringue powder to make a recipe of royal icing. Split the recipe into the three small bowls.

3. With a toothpick, add a drop of black icing color to one bowl of royal icing, and mix well. Cover the bowl with a towel until you use the icing.

4. With a toothpick, add a drop of green icing color to another small bowl of royal icing, and mix well. Again, cover the bowl with a towel.

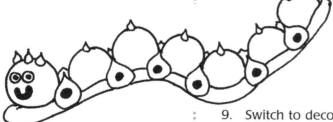

5. With a toothpick, add yellow icing color to the third bowl, and mix well. Cover the bowl with the last towel.

6. Work quickly and put the yellow icing into a decorator's bag with coupler and tip #12.

7. Squeeze the icing in a zigzag pattern onto the cardboard, working from one end to the other.

8. Quickly push all the gumballs into the icing, side-by-side.

9. Switch to decorating tip #5 and squeeze blobs of yellow icing on one side of the caterpillar at the bottom edge of the gumballs.

10. Fill another decorating bag with green icing along with coupler and tip #3. Squeeze out dots in the center of the yellow blobs.

11. Using decorating tip #3, place a dot of yellow icing on top of each gumball, except put two to three dots on the top of an end gumball. This will be the head.

12. Still using decorating tip #3 and the yellow icing, dot two eyes on the head.

13. Fill the third decorating bag with the black icing along with coupler and tip #2. Dot pupils onto the yellow eyes, and add a mouth.

14. Let the caterpillar sit for a few hours to harden.

15. This is an edible caterpillar. The children simply pull their gumballs off the foil cardboard to eat.

Note: You will have plenty of royal icing to make more Caterpillar Gums.

126

INGREDIENTS AND SUPPLIES FOR ANIMAL SWEETS

DOGGIE ROLL (K-6)

Five Hersheys Kisses® (red)

Smarties® candy roll

Glue gun

Two 7 mm moving eyes

1-inch square red felt

Scissors

5 mm black pom-pom

1-inch piece pipe cleaner (any color)

EASY DINOSASUR ICE CREAM SANDWICH (K-6)

½ cup ice cream (any flavor)

Butter knife

Two dinosaur graham crackers

GUMDROP TEDDY BEAR (K-6)

Knife

Large red gumdrop

Two red M&M's®

Meringue (ingredients below)

Decorating bag

Decorating coupler

Decorating tip, #4 or #5

Large green gumdrop

Two small green gumdrops

Two small yellow gumdrops

Small heart-shaped candy

Lollipop stick

Styrofoam® (used as a drying base)

Optional: A sandwich bag and Valentine ribbon

MERINGUE

Wilton® Meringue Powder Mix

Powdered sugar

Water

Mixer and bowl

Spoon or spatula

SWEET ANIMAL COOKIES (K-6)

Six animal cookies (3 pairs of matching cookies)

3 teaspoons pink or red canned frosting

Butter knife

SNAKE BITES (K-6)

Scissors

42 inches white curling ribbon

3 feet red plastic wrap

Six individual bags of Valentine candy

3-inch square green construction paper

½ x 2-inch red construction paper

Tacky glue

Black permanent marker

PUPPY TREATS (K-6)

½ cup butter (1 stick)

½ cup peanut butter

6-ounce bag semi-sweet chocolate chips

Medium saucepan or microwave bowl

Spoon or spatula

1 cup Cheerios®

9 cups rice cereal squares

Large bowl

2 cups powdered sugar

Ten small sandwich bags

Ten 5-inch pieces black curling ribbon

Ten 5-inch pieces red curling ribbon

Ten blank note cards

Scissors

Black permanent marker

Paper hole puncher

Optional: New, clean dog bowl and scoop.

CATERPILLAR GUM (K-6)

1½ x 4½ inch cardboard

2 x 5-inch red foil

Tape

Meringue (see ingredients on this page)

Three small bowls

Three toothpicks

Wilton® Black Icing Color

Wilton® Green Icing Color

Wilton® Yellow Icing Color

Three spoons

Three kitchen towels

Three decorating bags

Three decorating couplers

Decorating tips, #2, #3, #5, and #12

Seven small green gumballs

POST OFFICE SWEETS

VALENTINE PACKAGE (K-6)

INGREDIENTS AND SUPPLIES

White decorating gel

Chocolate square snack cake

Makes one package

Easy!

DIRECTIONS

1. Use the decorating gel to draw a ribbon and bow on the top and sides of the snack cake.
2. Draw hearts on the top of the cake.

SPECIAL DELIVERY DESSERTS (K-6)

INGREDIENTS AND SUPPLIES

Red construction paper

Scissors

Black permanent marker

Class list

Two Valentine containers

10.75-ounce frozen pound cake

Knife

Platter

3 cups fresh sliced strawberries

1 cup fresh blueberries

Valentine candy (Post Office theme)

Three serving bowls

Three serving spoons

Plates (one per child)

Plastic spoons (one per child)

Whipped cream

Makes 10 desserts

DIRECTIONS

1. Cut the construction paper into small pieces, one per student.
2. Use the permanent marker to write each student's name on his own piece of paper. Place boys' names into the first Valentine container (marked for boys) and girls' names into the second container (marked for girls).
3. Slice the pound cake into ten equal pieces and place them on the platter.
4. Place the strawberries, blueberries, and Valentine candy into their own bowls with serving spoons.
5. Set up the plates, spoons, pound cake, fruit, and candy "cafeteria style."
6. Place the Valentine containers at the end of the "cafeteria line."
7. Have the boys come up to the dessert line. Each takes a plate and spoon, then proceeds through the line to make a Special Delivery Dessert. They each take one slice of pound cake, top it with blueberries and/or strawberries, squirt whipped cream on top, and then garnish it with Valentine candy.
8. When a boy makes it to the end of the line, he draws a name from the girls' Valentine container. He will then deliver his special dessert to that girl.
9. The boys then sit down and wait for their own special deliveries.
10. Then the girls go through the dessert line and repeat the process, choosing from the boys' container, and serving their Special Delivery Desserts to the boys.
11. The children wait to eat until everyone has been served.

Note: If boys and girls are not equal in number, choose one boy or girl to go through the line a second time.

CUTE CANDY MAILMAN (K-6)

INGREDIENTS AND SUPPLIES

Three pretzel sticks

Two large black gumdrops

Red Valentine jelly heart

Knife

Two red licorice bites

Chocolate decorating gel

Makes one mailman

DIRECTIONS

1. Insert one end of a pretzel stick into the top of a gumdrop, and the other end into the tip of the jelly heart.

2. Use the knife to slit open one end of each licorice bite, and insert one pretzel stick into each slit.

3. Wiggle both pretzel sticks into the jelly heart, one on each side, to form the mailman's arms.

4. Dot two eyes on the wide part of the jelly heart with the decorating gel.

5. Place the flat end of the last gumdrop on the table and slice it horizontally, in half.

6. Then slice the top of the gumdrop horizontally, in half. Discard the bottom portion.

7. Take the top of the gumdrop and carefully push it into the bottom portion of the gumdrop, to form a cap.

8. Carefully attach the cap on top of the jelly heart (head).

Note: Black gumdrops look the best but you may experiment with other-colored gumdrops.

CHOCOLATE MESSAGE (K-6)

INGREDIENTS AND SUPPLIES

Chocolate candy bar

Brown decorating gel

Makes one message

DIRECTIONS

1. Unwrap the chocolate bar.

2. Use the gel to write a Valentine saying on the bar. Let it dry a day or so.

Who was taller, George Washington or Abraham Lincoln?

George Washington was 6'2" and Abraham Lincoln was 6'4". So, the answer is Lincoln, who was 14 1/2 Hershey's® bars, placed end-to-end, tall.

POST OFFICE SWEETS

POST OFFICE CUPCAKE (K-6)

INGREDIENTS AND SUPPLIES

Wrapped Valentine sucker

White frosted cupcake (homemade or store-bought)

Decorating Decors sugar nonpareils

12 to 15 small conversation candy hearts

Makes one cupcake

DIRECTIONS

1. Unwrap the Valentine sucker and place the stick in the center of the cupcake, just enough to hold it in place.
2. Sprinkle nonpareils on top of the cupcake.
3. Place the tips of the conversation hearts, side-by-side, around the cupcake edge.

What makes a school Valentine party fun?

"Giving people Valentines and reading Valentines that your friends give you. I also like getting candy, cupcakes and singing Valentines."
Jill Stephens, Age 11

Note: This school conducts a unique fundraiser in conjunction with Valentine's Day. The children pay 25¢ to send a cupcake to a friend. It is delivered on Valentine's Day. Parents bake the cupcakes and send them in. Parents and volunteers deliver them — it's a great moneymaker. Also, for $1.00, the principal will dress up and deliver a "singing valentine" to a friend.

VALENTINE SUNDAES WITH A SPECIAL MESSAGE (K-6)

INGREDIENTS AND SUPPLIES

Scissors

White paper

Red permanent marker

Pepperidge Farm® Pirouettes (one per child)

Serving bowls

Serving spoons

Ice cream

Assorted ice cream toppings

Sliced bananas

Slices strawberries

Crushed pineapple

Maraschino cherries

Whipped cream

Nuts

Plastic bowls (one per child)

Plastic spoons (one per child)

Modify this recipe to serve the entire class

DIRECTIONS

1. Cut out one heart per child from the white paper.
2. Write special messages on the hearts with the red permanent marker, roll them up, and slip one into each pirouette cookie.
3. Use some of these special messages or make up your own:

This is your lucky day	You are special
Kindness will come your way	Someone wants to be your friend
You'll soon be first	Someone loves you

4. Place the ice cream sundae items into bowls, and let the children create their own sundaes. Each child gets one special cookie with a message.

INGREDIENTS AND SUPPLIES FOR POST OFFICE SWEETS

VALENTINE PACKAGE (K-6)

- White decorating gel
- Chocolate square snack cake

SPECIAL DELIVERY DESSERTS (K-6)

- Red construction paper
- Scissors
- Black permanent marker
- Class list
- Two Valentine containers
- 10.75-ounce frozen pound cake
- Knife
- Platter
- 3 cups fresh sliced strawberries
- 1 cup fresh blueberries
- Valentine candy (Post Office theme)
- Three serving bowls
- Three serving spoons
- Plates (one per child)
- Plastic spoons (one per child)
- Whipped cream

CUTE CANDY MAILMAN (K-6)

- Three pretzel sticks
- Two large black gumdrops
- Red Valentine jelly heart
- Knife
- Two red licorice bites
- Chocolate decorating gel

CHOCOLATE MESSAGE (K-6)

- Chocolate candy bar
- Brown decorating gel

POST OFFICE CUPCAKE (K-6)

- Wrapped Valentine sucker
- White frosted cupcake (homemade or store-bought)
- Decorating Decors sugar nonpareils
- 12-15 small conversation candy hearts

VALENTINE SUNDAES WITH A SPECIAL MESSAGE (K-6)

- Scissors
- White paper
- Red permanent marker
- Pepperidge Farm® Pirouettes (one per child)
- Serving bowls
- Serving spoons
- Ice cream
- Assorted ice cream toppings
- Sliced bananas
- Slices strawberries
- Crushed pineapple
- Maraschino cherries
- Whipped cream
- Nuts
- Plastic bowls (one per child)
- Plastic spoons (one per child)

FEBRUARY & PRESIDENTS' SWEETS

WASHINGTON'S CUPCAKES (K-6)

INGREDIENTS AND SUPPLIES

Cake mix (any flavor)

Valentine cupcake liners

Cupcake baking pan

16-ounce pink or red canned frosting

Decorating bag

Decorating coupler

Decorating tip, #16

Spoon or spatula

Two 21-ounce cans cherry pie filling

Makes 24 to 28 cupcakes (2/3 full)

DIRECTIONS

1. Bake the cupcakes using the directions on the box, and let cool.
2. Put the frosting into the decorator's bag, coupler and tip already in place.
3. Decorate only the outer edges of the cupcakes with a star design, leaving the middle unfrosted.
4. Scoop pie filling onto the center of the cupcake.

Tip: Transfer the cupcakes to the school, then add the filling.

FIRST PRESIDENT'S DESSERT (K-6)

INGREDIENTS AND SUPPLIES

Knife

Large black gumdrop

Two pretzel sticks

Two Little Debbie® Swiss cake rolls

Makes 2 desserts

At age 6, George Washington did indeed chop at some of his father's cherry tree with a hatchet. And yes, he did tell his dad the truth, that he had done it.

Cool!

DIRECTIONS

1. Slice the gumdrop vertically in half, and flatten the two halves slightly.
2. Push one end of a pretzel stick onto the narrow end of one gumdrop-half, to form a hatchet.
3. Lay the hatchet on top of a cake roll as if chopping it.
4. Repeat the above steps to make the second dessert, using the other half of the gumdrop.

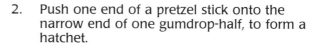

ABRAHAM LINCOLN'S LOG CABIN (K-6)

INGREDIENTS AND SUPPLIES

Chocolate sandwich cookies

Zippered sandwich bag

Rolling pin

Three graham crackers

Butter knife

Peanut butter

Pretzel sticks

4-inch square cardboard

Optional: Miscellaneous candy

Makes one cabin

DIRECTIONS

1. Put the cookies in the sandwich bag and close it. Crush with the rolling pin and set aside.

2. Break two graham crackers apart to make four equal squares.

3. Lay all four graham crackers flat, spread with the peanut butter, and "glue" pretzel sticks close together on each cracker, for the log's sides.

4. With the logs horizontal, and on the outside, put the four sides of the cabin together, "gluing" the corners with the peanut butter. "Glue" the cabin onto the center of the cardboard and freeze at least 15 minutes.

5. Break the third graham cracker in half, spread with peanut butter and "glue" pretzel pieces close together on both crackers. These will make the roof.

6. Very carefully, spread a heavy layer of peanut butter around the top of the cabin and "glue on" the roof. Be sure to "glue" the roof together at its peak.

7. Spread a thin layer of peanut butter onto the cardboard around the cabin. Sprinkle the crushed cookies on top of the peanut butter for the ground around the cabin. Then refreeze. Serve the log cabin immediately after taking it out of the freezer, or it might collapse.

Optional: Decorate with candy to make a door and smoke stack.

Tip: After Step #3, transfer to the school and assemble, then freeze using the school's freezer. Get permission to use the school's freezer first.

VALENTINE TREE (K-6)

INGREDIENTS AND SUPPLIES

Tree wreath (found at craft stores)

Scissors

Valentine jelly hearts

Allow 2 to 3 hearts per child

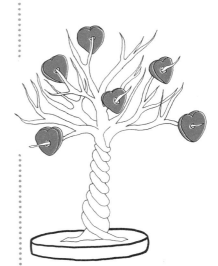

DIRECTIONS

1. Shape the branches to your liking, trimming some shorter with the scissors if you wish.

2. Stick the gummy hearts onto the tree branches, arranging where needed.

3. If the tree branches are too weak to hold the hearts, twist several branches together before sliding the hearts onto them.

Note: A tree wreath consists of wire branches twisted in a tube shape. You untwist the branches to your liking. Easter is a popular time to find these wreaths, used to hang miniature Easter eggs. Years ago, you could find tree wreaths made of plastic, used to hold olives, cheese, candy, etc. If you're lucky maybe a grandmother has one — ask around!

HAPPY VALENTINE'S DAY COOKIES (K-6)

INGREDIENTS AND SUPPLIES

Mixer and bowl

Spoon or spatula

½ cup shortening

¼ cup butter

Two eggs

1 cup sugar

1 teaspoon vanilla

2½ cups all-purpose flour

1/4 teaspoon salt

1 teaspoon baking powder

Rolling pin

Heart cookie cutter

Glaze (ingredients and recipe below)

Pastry brush

Cookie sheet

Decorating gel (any color)

Makes 15 large cookies or 24 small cookies

GLAZE:

Mixer and bowl

1 cup powdered sugar

1 tablespoon vanilla

1 tablespoon water

Food coloring (any color)

Spoon or spatula

COOKIE DIRECTIONS:

1. Cream the shortening, butter, eggs, sugar, and vanilla together.
2. Sift the flour, salt, and baking powder together.
3. Blend the flour mixture into the shortening mixture.
4. Refrigerate the dough for one hour.
5. Pre-heat oven to 400°
6. Roll the dough ⅛ inch thick on a lightly floured counter.
7. Cut with the heart cookie cutter and bake on an ungreased cookie sheet at 400° for 6 to 8 minutes or until lightly brown. Cool.
8. Spread the glaze on top of each cookie.
9. Use the decorating gel to outline the heart shape on each cookie. Then write the words "Happy Valentine's Day," with one word per cookie.
10. Give each child three cookies to say "Happy Valentine's Day."

GLAZE DIRECTIONS:

1. Blend the sugar, vanilla, and water in the bowl.
2. Stir in 2 to 3 drops of the food coloring.
3. If the glaze seems too thick, add ½ table-spoon of water at a time, being careful not to thin it too much.

INGREDIENTS AND SUPPLIES FOR FEBRUARY & PRESIDENTS' SWEETS

WASHINGTON'S CUPCAKES (K-6)

- Cake mix (any flavor)
- Valentine cupcake liners
- Cupcake baking pan
- 16-ounce pink or red canned frosting
- Decorating bag
- Decorating coupler
- Decorating tip, #16
- Spoon or spatula
- Two 21-ounce cans cherry pie filling

FIRST PRESIDENT'S DESSERT (K-6)

- Knife
- Large black gumdrop
- Two pretzel sticks
- Two Little Debbie® Swiss cake rolls

ABRAHAM LINCOLN'S LOG CABIN (K-6)

- Chocolate sandwich cookies
- Zippered sandwich bag
- Rolling pin
- Three graham crackers
- Butter knife
- Peanut butter
- Pretzel sticks
- 4-inch square cardboard
- *Optional: Miscellaneous candy*

VALENTINE TREE (K-6)

- Tree wreath (found at craft stores)
- Scissors
- Valentine jelly hearts

HAPPY VALENTINE'S DAY COOKIES (K-6)

- Mixer and bowl
- Spoon or spatula
- ½ cup shortening
- ¼ cup butter
- Two eggs
- 1 cup sugar
- 1 teaspoon vanilla
- 2½ cups all-purpose flour
- ¼ teaspoon salt
- 1 teaspoon baking powder
- Rolling pin
- Heart cookie cutter
- Glaze (ingredients and recipe below)
- Pastry brush
- Cookie sheet
- Decorating gel (any color)

GLAZE

- Mixer and bowl
- 1 cup powdered sugar
- 1 tablespoon vanilla
- 1 tablespoon water
- Food coloring (any color)
- Spoon or spatula

ALL-TIME FAVORITE SWEETS

ICE CREAM IN A GUTTER (K-6)

INGREDIENTS AND SUPPLIES

10-foot new plastic gutter (found at home-improvement stores)

2 cups ice cream (per child)

Ice cream scoop

Two cans whipped cream

Maraschino cherries (one per child)

Assorted candy

Bowls (one per child)

Plastic spoons (one per child)*

You can comfortably fit twenty children at the gutter, each getting a 6-inch section

Tell us about your best room party.

"We have had great success with the make-your-own sundae bar."
Stephanie Major
Franktown, Colorado

Caution: Due to health reasons, do not use painted gutters.

Chocolate sprinkles on spoons are a big hit with the children. You can find the recipe on page 137.

DIRECTIONS

1. Wash and dry the gutter thoroughly.

2. Prepare this extra large sundae at school and work quickly. Do not transfer once assembled.

3. Scoop the ice cream into the gutter.

4. Decorate with whipped cream, cherries, and assorted candy. Serve immediately.

5. After everyone "ooh's and aah's," scoop the ice cream into their bowls and serve, or use the following variation.

Note: Most gutters sell in 10-foot sections. The home-improvement stores can cut gutters smaller if desired. They also sell gutter ends to hook onto the sides of the gutter. This can prevent the ice cream from leaking.

Variation: Children enjoy eating out of the gutter. To do so, leave a 3-inch gap between the servings to help eliminate health concerns.

VALENTINE SODA (K-6)

INGREDIENTS AND SUPPLIES

16-ounce red plastic cup

1 cup vanilla or strawberry ice cream

¾ cup strawberry pop

Whipped cream

Maraschino cherry

Two sugar-wafers

Pink flexible straw

Optional: Plastic spoon

Makes one soda

DIRECTIONS

1. Fill the plastic cup with the ice cream.

2. Pour in the strawberry pop. Do not stir.

3. Squirt some whipped cream on top of the soda.

4. Add the cherry on top, and stick in two sugar-wafers and a straw. Enjoy!

Optional: Include a spoon with the soda.

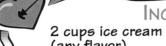

ICE CREAM IN A BAG (K-6)

INGREDIENTS AND SUPPLIES

2 cups ice cream
(any flavor)

Ice cream scoop

Zippered sandwich
bag

¼ cup crushed
cookies (any type)

¼ cup Valentine
candy

Two small paper
cups

Plastic spoon

Whipped cream

Maraschino cherry

Makes one ice cream bag

DIRECTIONS

1. Scoop the ice cream into the sandwich bag. Close and freeze until the party.
2. Put the crushed cookies and Valentine candy in their own paper cups.
3. At party time, each child gets an ice cream bag, a cup of cookies, a cup of candy, a spoon, and a cherry if he chooses (not all children like cherries).
4. The child can dump his "goodies" on top of the ice cream or wait for the whipped cream.
5. The child or parent can squirt whipped cream into the bag.

CHOCOLATE SPRINKLES ON SPOONS (K-6)

INGREDIENTS AND SUPPLIES

¹/₆ bar paraffin wax

Double boiler or microwave bowl

6-ounce bag semi-sweet
chocolate chips

2-ounce Hershey's® bar

Spoon or spatula

Red plastic spoons (one per
child)

5 ounces Decorating Decors
rainbow sprinkles

Styrofoam® square

*This recipe will easily coat
enough spoons for a large class.*

Great spoons to use with ice cream!

DIRECTIONS

1. Melt the paraffin wax in the double boiler or in a microwave.
2. Add the chocolate chips and Hershey's(r) bar and let melt, stirring often.
3. Dip a spoon into the chocolate mixture and raise it slowly. Hold the spoon over the pan for a few seconds to let any excess chocolate drip off.
4. Immediately shake the sprinkles onto the chocolate part of the spoon.
5. Stick the handle of the spoon into the Styrofoam® to let the chocolate harden.
6. Repeat Steps 1 to 5 until you have enough spoons for the whole class.

Tip: Do not make more than one day ahead of time.

ALL-TIME FAVORITE SWEETS

Rose Mason is the kitchen manager of Ralph Moody Elementary and is happy to share her recipe with us.

Note: Rose likes to pipe a border on the cookies first with her buttercream icing. Then she brushes on the colored corn syrup. She lets them air dry for at least 30 to 60 minutes before wrapping, allowing more time if needed due to humidity.

POPULAR VALENTINE SUGAR COOKIES (K-6)

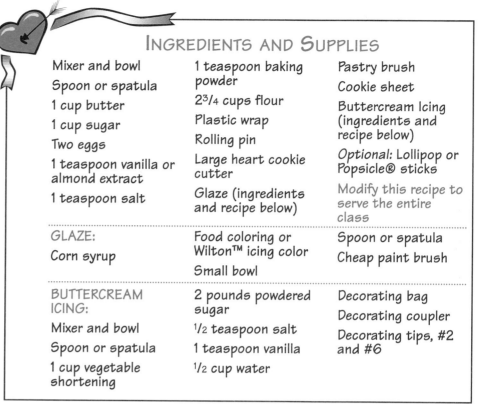

INGREDIENTS AND SUPPLIES

Mixer and bowl	1 teaspoon baking powder	Pastry brush
Spoon or spatula	2³/4 cups flour	Cookie sheet
1 cup butter	Plastic wrap	Buttercream Icing (ingredients and recipe below)
1 cup sugar	Rolling pin	
Two eggs	Large heart cookie cutter	*Optional:* Lollipop or Popsicle® sticks
1 teaspoon vanilla or almond extract		Modify this recipe to serve the entire class
1 teaspoon salt	Glaze (ingredients and recipe below)	

GLAZE:	Food coloring or Wilton™ icing color	Spoon or spatula
Corn syrup	Small bowl	Cheap paint brush

BUTTERCREAM ICING:	2 pounds powdered sugar	Decorating bag
Mixer and bowl	1/2 teaspoon salt	Decorating coupler
Spoon or spatula	1 teaspoon vanilla	Decorating tips, #2 and #6
1 cup vegetable shortening	1/2 cup water	

COOKIE DIRECTIONS:

1. Cream the butter, sugar, eggs, and vanilla together. Rose says that children like the almond flavor extract best!

2. Add the salt and baking powder, and mix thoroughly.

3. Slowly add the flour and mix thoroughly.

4. Cover tightly with plastic wrap and store in the refrigerator for at least four hours or overnight.

5. Preheat oven to 350°.

6. Roll the dough 1/4-inch thick on a lightly floured counter. Cut with the heart cookie cutter.

7. You can decide here to brush the glaze onto the cookies before baking, or wait until after baking them.

8. Place on ungreased cookie sheet and bake 6 to 10 minutes or until lightly brown.

Optional: Wet a lollipop or Popsicle® stick and slide it into the tip of the heart cookie before baking.

GLAZE DIRECTIONS:

1. Pour corn syrup and drops of food coloring into a bowl. Make the color as dark or as light as you wish. Make sure you mix the syrup and food coloring well. *Caution:* Be careful, the color does not come out of clothes.

2. With the brush, paint the glaze onto cool cookies, and let dry for at least 30 to 60 minutes.

BUTTERCREAM ICING DIRECTIONS:

1. Beat the shortening, sugar, salt, vanilla, and water together. The longer you beat the icing with the mixer, the better.

2. Add more sugar to make the icing thicker, or more water to make the icing thinner.

INGREDIENTS AND SUPPLIES FOR ALL-TIME FAVORITE SWEETS

ICE CREAM IN A GUTTER (K-6)

10-foot new plastic gutter (found at home-improvement stores)

2 cups ice cream (per child)

Ice cream scoop

Two cans whipped cream

Maraschino cherries (one per child)

Assorted candy

Bowls (one per child)

Plastic spoons (one per child)

VALENTINE SODA (K-6)

16-ounce red plastic cup

1 cup vanilla or strawberry ice cream

3/4 cup strawberry pop

Whipped cream

Maraschino cherry

Two sugar-wafers

Pink flexible straw

Optional: Plastic spoon

ICE CREAM IN A BAG (K-6)

2 cups ice cream (any flavor)

Ice cream scoop

Zippered sandwich bag

1/4 cup crushed cookies (any type)

1/4 cup Valentine candy

Two small paper cups

Plastic spoon

Whipped cream

Maraschino cherry

CHOCOLATE SPRINKLES ON SPOONS (K-6)

1/6 bar paraffin wax

Double boiler or microwave bowl

6-ounce bag semi-sweet chocolate chips

2-ounce Hershey's® bar

Spoon or spatula

Red plastic spoons (one per child)

5 ounces Decorating Decors rainbow sprinkles

Styrofoam® square

POPULAR VALENTINE SUGAR COOKIES (K-6)

Mixer and bowl

Spoon or spatula

1 cup butter

1 cup sugar

Two eggs

1 teaspoon vanilla or almond extract

1 teaspoon salt

1 teaspoon baking powder

2 3/4 cups flour

Plastic wrap

Rolling pin

Large heart cookie cutter

Glaze (ingredients below)

Pastry brush

Cookie sheet

Buttercream Icing (ingredients below)

Optional: Lollipop or Popsicle® sticks

GLAZE

Corn syrup

Food coloring or Wilton™ icing color

Small bowl

Spoon or spatula

Cheap paint brush

BUTTERCREAM ICING

Mixer and bowl

Spoon or spatula

1 cup vegetable shortening

2 pounds powdered sugar

1/2 teaspoon salt

1 teaspoon vanilla

1/2 cup water

Decorating bag

Decorating coupler

Decorating tips, #2 and #6

CHAPTER FIVE
DRINKS

HELPFUL HINTS

HELPFUL HINTS FOR DRINKS

1. Check all recipes to see if there are any preparations to be done ahead of time.
2. Use red licorice for straws.
3. Cut heart shapes out of construction paper and punch holes in them to slide onto straws.
4. Freeze items into ice cubes, such as red hots, heart-shaped candy, red M&M's™, or strawberries. *Be careful* when freezing small items into ice cubes – younger children may choke.
5. Freeze club soda or seltzer into heart-shaped ice cube trays. Let kids place them into punch so they can watch them fizz.
6. When using maraschino cherries for garnish, lay them on paper towels to remove excess juice.
7. Maraschino cherry juice can be added in place of grenadine in the Kitty Cocktail recipe.
8. Dampen the rim of a clear cup with water. Dip this moist rim into a dish of sugar. Fill it with your favorite drink, preferably pink or red for Valentine's Day.
9. Any combination of cut-up fruit on a small skewer adds to the drink's fun and flavor.
10. A fast and quick Valentine beverage could be pink lemonade or Hawaiian Punch®.
11. For any drink, add a strawberry fan* to the drink edge and use a pink straw.
12. Choose red, pink, or Valentine's Day cups to enhance the appearance of your drink. Just make sure they're not glass.
13. Freeze strawberry frozen yogurt or strawberry pop into heart-shaped ice cube trays, and add to the drinks instead of ice cubes.
14. Experiment with different blends of fruit juices and pop that, of course, are pink or red.
15. Make sure your punch bowl is big enough. Most recipes make approximately two gallons.

* Strawberry sliced thin with stem attached, then spread out.

DRINK INTRODUCTION
How to Use This Chapter

There are a few drink recipes that serve only one. All other recipes will provide 28 one-cup servings, 37 three-quarter cup servings or 56 half-cup servings. Typically, fifth and sixth graders will drink one cup or more. Second, third, and fourth graders need a three-quarter cup serving, whereas a half cup is plenty for kindergartners and first graders.

Are you looking at these figures thinking that your child could drink more? I agree, they can, but my experience as a classroom party planner has taught me that most children don't. They are just too busy with all of the excitement that a lot of drinks go into the trash. However, if it is a very hot day, plan larger servings. Don't forget that the parent volunteers attending the party and the classroom teacher will want to have some drinks as well. Be sure to read Helpful Hints for Drinks on the opposite page. Cheers!

DRINKS

HEART DRINK
FROZEN HEARTACHE (K-6)

INGREDIENTS AND SUPPLIES

Capri Sun® Juice Drink	Bowl
Knife	Plastic spoon
Paper towel	Straw
Cheese grater	Makes one drink

A popular drink with my children. Thanks, Michelle and Nick!

DIRECTIONS

1. Freeze the juice overnight.
2. Use your knife to slice the top of the bag open, one side at a time. (Do not use scissors to cut straight through.)
3. Slide the juice out of the wrapper and secure with a paper towel.
4. Grate the juice into the bowl. Serve immediately with a spoon. If the juice melts, use a straw.

Note: Older children like to grate their own frozen juice.

143

DRINKS

CUPID DRINK

TART & TANGY CUPID PUNCH (K-6)

INGREDIENTS AND SUPPLIES

Three 2-liter bottles of ginger ale

One 1-liter (82 ounces) bottle of cranberry juice

Punch bowl and ladle

Red cellophane frills toothpicks (one per drink)

Pineapple chunks (one per drink)

Clear cups

Serves the entire class

DIRECTIONS

1. Pour ginger ale and juice into the punch bowl. Stir.

2. Push a toothpick through each wide end of a pineapple chunk to form Cupid's arrow.

3. Serve juice with one toothpick arrow.

LOVE & FRIENDSHIP DRINK

SQUEEZE & HUG DRINK (K-6)

INGREDIENTS AND SUPPLIES

Scissors

Red construction paper

Paper hole puncher

Black permanent marker

12-inch red pipe cleaner

Glue gun

Squeezit® fruit drink

1-inch square red craft foam

Makes one drink

DIRECTIONS

1. Cut a 3-inch heart from construction paper.

2. Punch two holes into the bottom of the heart, side-by-side.

3. Draw a face onto the heart with the black permanent marker.

4. Slide the pipe cleaner through the holes, so both ends come out behind the face.

5. Attach the heart face to the top of the bottle with a dab of glue.

6. Wrap the pipe cleaner (arms) around the front of the Squeezit® (body) and cross its arms.

7. Cut two small hearts (hands) from the craft foam, glue onto the ends of the pipe cleaner.

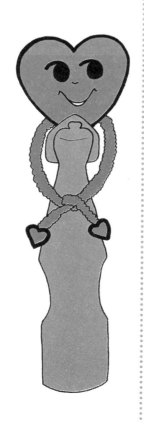

144

ANIMAL DRINK

KITTY COCKTAIL (K-6)

INGREDIENTS AND SUPPLIES

Measuring cups

Three 2-liter bottles of ginger ale

Clear cups

One 32-ounce bottle of grenadine

Knife

Four to five oranges

Maraschino cherries (one per drink)

Red cellophane frills toothpicks (one per drink)

Serves the entire class

A favorite among children also called a Shirley Temple.

DIRECTIONS

1. Pour 1 cup (8 ounces) of ginger ale into each cup. Add 1 ounce (¹/₈ cup) of grenadine. Stir.

2. Cut each orange into six to eight slices.

3. Fold an orange slice around a cherry and slide the toothpick through the center to secure. Place garnish in cup.

POST OFFICE DRINK

POST OFFICE DELIGHT (K-6)

INGREDIENTS AND SUPPLIES

12-ounce can frozen lemonade

12-ounce can frozen pineapple juice

Two packages cherry Kool-Aid®

1½ cups sugar

4 quarts water

1 quart ginger ale

Punch bowl and ladle

2½ cups pineapple chunks

2½ cups frozen or fresh strawberries

Red plastic cups

Serves the entire class

Any postman would enjoy a cup of this punch during the busy Valentine season.

DIRECTIONS

1. Pour all ingredients into a punch bowl except the fruit. Stir well.

2. Add the pineapples and strawberries.

3. Serve the punch with the fruit.

145

DRINKS

FEBRUARY & PRESIDENTS' DRINK

YUMMY PRESIDENTIAL DAIQUIRIS (K-6)

INGREDIENTS AND SUPPLIES

Two 12-ounce cans frozen lemonade

Two 12-ounce cans water

4 pints frozen or fresh strawberries (8 cups)

10 to 12 cups ice

Blender

Clear cups

Red straws

Serves the entire class

DIRECTIONS

1. Add ½ can (6 ounces) lemonade, ½ can water, and 1 pint (2 cups) of strawberries into a blender.

2. Fill ice to the top of the blender and blend until smooth and slushy. This recipe needs to be made in several batches, so repeat steps 1 and 2 until ingredients are gone.

3. Pour into clear cups with straws.

Note: If using frozen strawberries, decrease the amount of ice.

INGREDIENTS AND SUPPLIES FOR DRINKS

FROZEN HEARTACHE (K-6)

- Capri Sun® Juice Drink
- Knife
- Paper towel
- Cheese grater
- Bowl
- Plastic spoon
- Straw

TART & TANGY CUPID PUNCH (K-6)

- Three 2-liter bottles of ginger ale
- One 1-liter (82 ounces) bottle of cranberry juice
- Punch bowl and ladle
- Red cellophane frills toothpicks (one per drink)
- Pineapple chunks (one per drink)
- Clear cups

SQUEEZE & HUG DRINK (K-6)

- Scissors
- Red construction paper
- Paper hole puncher
- Black permanent marker
- 12-inch red pipe cleaner
- Glue gun
- Squeezit® fruit drink
- 1-inch square red craft foam

KITTY COCKTAIL (K-6)

- Measuring cups
- Three 2-liter bottles of ginger ale
- Clear cups
- One 32-ounce bottle of grenadine
- Knife
- Four to five oranges
- Maraschino cherries (one per drink)
- Red cellophane frills toothpicks (one per drink)

POST OFFICE DELIGHT (K-6)

- 12-ounce can frozen lemonade
- 12-ounce can frozen pineapple juice
- Two packages cherry Kool-Aid®
- 1½ cups sugar
- 4 quarts water
- 1 quart ginger ale
- Punch bowl and ladle
- 2½ cups pineapple chunks
- 2½ cups frozen or fresh strawberries
- Red plastic cups

YUMMY PRESIDENTIAL DAQUIRIES (K-6)

- Two 12-ounce cans frozen lemonade
- Two 12-ounce cans water
- 4 pints frozen or fresh strawberries
- 10 to 12 cups ice
- Blender
- Clear cups
- Red straws

CHAPTER SIX
VALENTINE BOXES

HELPFUL HINTS

HELPFUL HINTS FOR VALENTINE BOXES

1.   When undecided what type of box to make, choose a theme — it gives you direction.

2.   There is no idea too wild.

3.   Save different kinds of boxes, such as oatmeal containers, cereal boxes, tissue boxes, and flip-top boot boxes. They make some rather unique Valentine boxes rather than the traditional shoebox.

4.   Bags and envelopes can also be turned into some great Valentine containers.

5.   You'd be surprised how many items lying around the house can be used for boxes. Be creative!

6.   When putting together boxes, test which glue works best — tacky glue or glue sticks (glue gun).

7.   Do not forget to cut a slit for Valentines to be deposited, as well as a way to retrieve your cards.

8.   There may be times you'll need to shake Valentines out of the container to retrieve them, or you may choose to cut the box open.

9.   Valentines can be a card, message, gift or candy.

10. Building Valentine boxes can be a great family project!

11. When personalizing a box with another word after your name add 's to your name such as Donna's school or Rose's house.

This chapter is compiled of award-winning boxes
from elementary school-age children.

We would like to thank all of the children
and the judges who participated.

HEART BOXES

KATHRYN'S VALENTINE BOX

SUPPLIES

Scissors

Shoebox with lid

White paper

Tape

Pink construction paper

Red construction paper

Glue

Red-hot heart candy

Queen of Hearts playing card

King of Hearts playing card

Confetti hearts

By
Kathryn Lohringel
Grade 4
Mark Hopkins Elementary
Littleton, Colorado

DIRECTIONS

1. Cut a slit in the lid of the shoebox to deposit the Valentines.

2. Wrap the shoebox, top and bottom separately, with white paper. Tape to secure.

3. Cut out two pink hearts and two red hearts, and glue them to the front side of the box. Glue four heart candies onto these hearts.

4. Cut out assorted red and pink hearts, and glue them to the back edge of the box so they are standing up.

5. Glue the Queen of Hearts and King of Hearts playing cards onto the top of the box.

6. Using the confetti hearts, spell out your name and glue it on top of the box underneath the slit.

HEART BOXES

By
Lynette Simpson
Grade 2
Mark Hopkins Elementary
Littleton, Colorado

HEART VALENTINE BOX

SUPPLIES

Scissors

Empty heart-shaped chocolate box

Red spray paint

Glue gun

4 x 5-inch facial tissue box

Cardboard

Two straws

White paper

Gold spray paint

Lace

Optional: Gold paint marker

DIRECTIONS

1. Cut off the sides of the heart-shaped box, so you have two flat heart shapes.

2. Spray paint the bottoms of the hearts and the tissue box red. Let dry.

3. Glue the hearts onto opposite sides of the tissue box.

4. Glue a triangle-shaped piece of cardboard to one end of a straw to form the arrow tip. Glue white paper feathers to the opposite end of the straw to form the shaft. Cut the straw into three pieces, cutting the center portion smaller than the ends. Repeat to make a second arrow. Set aside.

5. Spray paint the arrow pieces gold and let them dry.

6. Glue lace around both hearts.

7. Glue the arrow pieces onto the hearts at an angle, as shown in the illustration.

8. The Valentines are deposited into the tissue box.

Optional: Also in the illustration, you will see the embossed rose that was originally on the box. If your box is similar, you can add a cute saying such as "LOVE STRUCK!" on the other side of the box.

PAT'S PINK PAD

SUPPLIES

Tape

Cardboard box with flaps

Shoebox with lid

Scissors

Cotton balls

Glue gun

Bright pink construction paper

Red permanent marker

White construction paper

Light pink construction paper

Conversation candy hearts

By
Pat Botkins
Grade 5
Mark Hopkins Elementary
Littleton, Colorado

DIRECTIONS

1. Tape the bottom of the box closed.

2. Bring the top flaps almost together (leave enough room to fit in the shoebox lid) and tape.

3. Take the shoebox lid and fit it into the opening at the top of the box. Tape in place.

4. Cut a chimney from the shoebox. Tape on top of the shoebox lid.

5. Stuff cotton balls into the chimney to look like smoke, and glue if needed.

6. Wrap the entire box, including the chimney, with bright pink construction paper, and tape to secure.

7. Draw a door and window onto the box with the red permanent marker.

8. Draw red hearts on top of the roof.

9. Cut a slit in the door to slide Valentines through.

10. Cut enough hearts from white construction paper and spell out your name, and the word "Pad," one letter per heart.

11. Cut four hearts from light pink construction paper and write the word "Pink," one letter per heart.

12. Glue "your name" and "Pink Pad" near the window and door.

13. Glue conversation hearts on the chimney, door, around the window, and on the hearts on top of the box.

HEART BOXES

CONVERSATION HEART CANDY BOX

By
Kelsey Antun
Grade 3
Mark Hopkins Elementary
Littleton, Colorado

SUPPLIES

Scissors

Empty heart-shaped chocolate box

10 inches 1/4" red ribbon

Glue

Gold heart-shaped doily

Child's picture

Sequins

Gold bow

Conversation candy hearts

20 inches Valentine's Day ribbon

DIRECTIONS

1. Cut a slit in the top, side of the heart-shaped box for the Valentines to slide through.

2. Use your scissors to poke a small hole on each side of the slit, and thread the ribbon through. Tie the ends together securely, to hang your box if desired.

3. Glue a doily on the top of the box then glue your picture to the doily. Glue sequins around the picture.

4. Glue a bow at the bottom of the doily.

5. Glue conversation hearts on the box, around the doily.

6. Cut the Valentine's Day ribbon into four pieces and glue from the bottom of the box.

PEARLS, ROSES, AND RHINESTONES

SUPPLIES

Double-sided tape	X-acto® knife	2 yards imitation pearls (found at craft and fabric stores)
Shoebox (boot size)	Assorted acrylic faceted stones	
Silver wrapping paper	Small gold heart-shaped doily	Two red silk roses (without stems)
Glue gun	Scissors	Valentine heart stickers
Pencil		

By
Kalyn Fong
Grade 4
Laura Ingalls Wilder Elementary
Littleton, Colorado

DIRECTIONS

1. Place double-sided tape on the top of the box lid. Wrap the lid tightly with silver wrapping paper, smoothing it out onto the tape as you go. Use a glue gun if necessary.

2. Repeat Step #1 for the box bottom.

3. On the underside of the box lid, draw a heart shape toward the right side. Using an X-acto® knife, carefully cut most of the heart out, leaving a 1½ inch straight line on the right side of the heart. This will be the hinge. When the lid is flipped over, the heart will end up on the left side of the box, with a left-sided hinge. Re-smooth the wrapping paper if needed.

4. Glue the stones in place around the top edges of the lid.

5. Glue a doily to the heart-shaped door on the top of the lid.

6. Cut a 6-inch strand of imitation pearls and glue to the right-hand side of the doily. This will be the handle of the door. Open the door to deposit the Valentines. Attach silk roses on top of the pearls to disguise any glue.

7. Cut the remaining pearls in half. This will give you two 33-inch strands.

8. Quickly place eight equally-spaced globs of glue on the front edge of the lid. Loop one strand of pearls from glue glob to glue glob across the front (each loop is approximately 4 inches long).

9. Repeat Step #8 for the back edge of the lid with the second strand of pearls.

10. Glue any leftover stones and Valentine heart stickers to the sides of the box.

SUPPLIES FOR HEART BOXES

KATHRYN'S VALENTINE BOX

Scissors
Shoebox with lid
White paper
Tape
Pink construction paper
Red construction paper

Glue
Red-hot heart candy
Queen of Hearts playing card
King of Hearts playing card
Confetti hearts

HEART VALENTINE BOX

Scissors
Empty heart-shaped chocolate box
Red spray paint
Glue gun
4 x 5-inch facial tissue box
Cardboard
Two straws
White paper
Gold spray paint
Lace
Optional: gold paint marker

PAT'S PINK PAD

Tape
Cardboard box with flaps
Shoebox with lid
Scissors
Cotton balls
Glue gun
Bright pink construction paper

Red permanent marker
White construction paper
Light pink construction paper
Conversation candy hearts

CONVERSATION HEART CANDY BOX

Scissors
Empty heart-shaped chocolate box
10 inches 1/4" red ribbon
Glue
Gold heart-shaped doily
Child's picture
Sequins
Gold bow
Conversation candy hearts
20 inches Valentine's Day ribbon

PEARLS, ROSES, AND RHINESTONES

Double-sided tape
Shoebox (boot size)
Silver wrapping paper
Glue gun
Pencil
X-acto® knife
Assorted acrylic faceted stones
Small gold heart-shaped doily

Scissors
2 yards imitation pearls (found at craft and fabric stores)
Two red silk roses (without stems)
Valentine heart stickers

CUPID BOXES

CUPID'S VALENTINE BOX

SUPPLIES

Picture of Cupid	Spray adhesive	White construction paper
Scissors	Ruler	
Two sheets red poster board	Glue	Glitter
		Optional: String

DIRECTIONS

1. Enlarge a picture of Cupid on a copy machine so the Cupid is 16 to 18 inches tall. (This will take two pieces of copy paper).

2. Cut out the Cupid and use it as a pattern to trace onto each sheet of red poster board.

3. Carefully cut out both Cupids. Use the spray adhesive to glue them together.

4. To make the quiver, cut an 8 x 11-inch piece of red poster board.

5. Fold 1 inch in on both 8-inch sides and on one 11-inch side of the poster board.

6. Clip the folded edge of the 11 inch side every 1 inch.

7. Bend the poster board into an arch, and trace a quiver bottom onto a scrap of red poster board. Glue the quiver bottom onto the clipped-side of the poster board.

8. Glue the folded edges of the quiver to the front of Cupid. The Valentines are deposited in the quiver.

9. Cut out a heart from the white construction paper and glue to the front of the quiver.

10. Glue glitter on Cupid's hair, wings, and arrow tip.

Optional: A string can be inserted through a hole in the top of the head to hang if desired.

Note: A quiver is a case for holding or carrying arrows.

By

Steven Christiansen

Kindergarten

Mark Hopkins Elementary

Littleton, Colorado

CUPID BOXES

CUPID BOXES

By
Alison Cavanaugh
Grade 3
Laura Ingalls Wilder
Elementary
Littleton, Colorado

CUPID TISSUE BOX

SUPPLIES

Tape

Cardboard box
(not a shoebox)

Decorative tissue
paper

Paint brush

Decoupage glue
(found in craft
stores)

X-acto® knife

Scissors

Button with shank

Glue gun

Ribbon

Cupid ornaments
(left over from
Christmas
decorations)

DIRECTIONS

1. Tape the box closed.

2. Cover the box with tissue paper and "paint" it with decoupage glue. Allow it to dry completely.

3. Using an X-acto® knife cut a three-sided "door" on top of the box. This is where Valentine cards will be deposited.

4. Punch a small hole in the door and attach the button with glue for the doorknob.

5. Make a bow out of ribbon and glue on top of the box, behind the door. Glue Cupid ornaments around the top edge of the box.

CUPID'S QUIVER

SUPPLIES

Red poster board

Stapler

Packaging tape (clear)

Paper hole puncher

Approximately 40 inches heavy white rope

Scissors

Red construction paper

Glue gun

24" wooden dowel

Optional:
Permanent markers and Valentine heart stickers

By
Wilhelminia Ripple
Littleton, Colorado

CUPID BOXES

DIRECTIONS

1. Roll the poster board lengthwise into a cylinder.

2. Staple and tape to hold in place.

3. Punch a hole on one side of the poster board, 4 inches from the bottom.

4. Bend the bottom of the quiver inward, just below the hole, to form a base. Tape securely.

5. Punch a hole 1 inch down from the top of the cylinder, on the same side as the bottom hole. Punch another hole, 1 inch down from the top, on the opposite side of the cylinder.

6. Knot one end of the rope and slip the opposite end of the rope into the quiver and through the bottom hole, so your knot is on the inside of the cylinder.

7. Slide the rope up the outside of the quiver and thread through the hole on the top. Then thread the rope across the inside of the quiver and through the opposite hole. Leave slack in the rope so you can carry the quiver. Knot the end of the rope.

8. Cut arrow feathers from red construction paper and glue to one end of the dowel, to make the arrow. Place the arrow into the quiver.

9. Valentines are deposited into the top of the quiver.

Optional: Personalize and decorate with Valentine heart stickers.

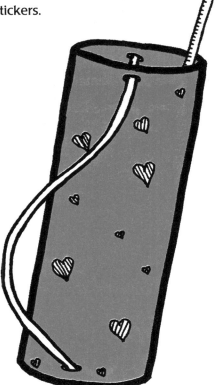

159

SUPPLIES FOR CUPID BOXES

CUPID'S VALENTINE BOX

- Picture of Cupid
- Scissors
- Two sheets red poster board
- Spray adhesive
- Ruler
- Glue
- White construction paper
- Glitter
- *Optional: String*

CUPID TISSUE BOX

- Tape
- Cardboard box (not a shoebox)
- Decorative tissue paper
- Paint brush
- Decoupage glue (found in craft stores)
- X-acto® knife
- Scissors
- Button with shank
- Glue gun
- Ribbon
- Cupid ornaments (left over from Christmas decorations)

CUPID'S QUIVER

- Red poster board
- Stapler
- Packaging tape (clear)
- Paper hole puncher
- Approximately 40 inches heavy white rope
- Scissors
- Red construction paper
- Glue gun
- 24" wooden dowel
- *Optional: Permanent markers and Valentine heart stickers*

Don't forget the camera and film.

LOVE & FRIENDSHIP BOXES

DIAMONDS ARE A GIRL'S BEST FRIEND

SUPPLIES

Tape	Glue gun	Imitation pearl strand
Small cardboard box	Scissors	Imitation diamond ring
Pink wrapping paper	Permanent markers	
	Imitation diamond studs	Four heart-stones

DIRECTIONS

1. Tape the box closed.

2. Cover the box with wrapping paper and glue to secure. Cut a slit in the top of the box for the Valentine cards to be deposited.

3. Using a permanent marker, write "Diamonds are a Girl's Best Friend" on the top of the box.

4. Glue imitation diamonds around the card slot.

5. Loop a strand of imitation pearls around the top side of the box and glue.

6. Draw a boy, girl, and trees on the front side of the box and color. Glue a small strand of imitation pearls to the bottom edge of the girl's dress.

7. Cut a small slit between the boy and girl's hands. Slide the ring into the slit and glue to secure.

8. Glue the heart stones to the top of the box, one in each corner.

By
Kelsey Schaecher
Grade 5
Mark Hopkins Elementary
Littleton, Colorado

MISSISSIPPI RIVER LOVE BOAT

SUPPLIES

- Large rectangular box with flip-top lid
- Scissors
- Stapler
- Tape
- Glue gun or craft glue
- Medium square box
- Small square box
- Three toilet paper rolls
- Lots of craft sticks broken in half
- 1/4" wooden dowel
- 5 x 16-inch poster board
- Spray paint (any color)
- Red permanent markers
- Valentine heart stickers
- Yarn or string (any color)

By
Clayton Wilbanks
Grade 3
Laura Ingalls Wilder Elementary
Littleton, Colorado

DIRECTIONS

1. Flip the lid open on the largest box.

2. Cut out one end panel from the large box. At the same end, cut along the bottom sides of the box, one-third of the length of the box.

3. Bring together the flaps you have just created, and staple or tape to form the pointed, or front end of the boat.

4. Again at the same end, cut the bottom of the box into a point. Flip the lid back on the box, and cut the top of the box to match the bottom.

5. Glue the medium box to the top of the large box. Glue the small box on the top of the medium box, leaving enough room to glue two toilet paper rolls standing up on top of the medium box, in front of the small box, as shown in the illustration.

6. Glue craft sticks around the tops of the large and medium boxes to form railings.

7. To make the paddle wheel, cut the dowel rod into three equal parts. Slide one part through a toilet paper roll. Glue the other parts onto the ends of the first dowel rod to form a u-shape. Roll the poster board strip around the toilet paper roll, on the indside of the "U" and staple or tape to secure.

8. Glue a few craft sticks inside the paddle wheel between the poster board and the toilet paper roll, to form spokes.

9. Poke two holes in the back of the boat, stick the dowel ends from the paddle wheel in the holes, and glue to secure.

10. Spray paint the entire boat and let dry.

11. Draw hearts on the lower railing with the red permanent marker and add Valentine heart stickers where desired.

12. Drape and glue yarn around the same railing.

13. Write "open," with arrows pointing up, on the side of the box that flips up. This shows where to deposit the Valentines.

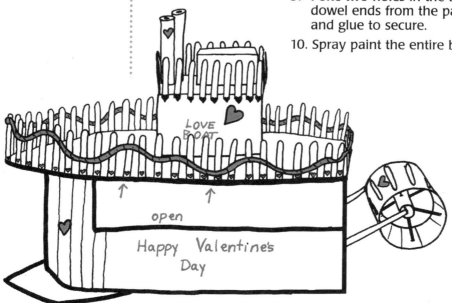

FRIENDS FOREVER

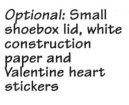

SUPPLIES

Large shoe box

Pink poster board

Glue

Last year's Valentine box lid

Scissors

White lace

Red construction paper

Clay dolls (handmade)

Clay bench (handmade)

1 x 3-inch white paper

Red permanent marker

Two silk roses (without stems)

Friendship sayings (from magazines, greeting cards, etc.)

Optional: Small shoebox lid, white construction paper and Valentine heart stickers

By
Allison Pelissier
Grade 5
Mark Hopkins Elementary
Littleton, Colorado

DIRECTIONS

1. Cover the entire box with pink poster board and glue in place.

2. Take the lid of last year's box and glue it to the top of the shoebox, in the middle. Cut a slit in the top of the box, if there was not one previously, to deposit Valentines.

3. Glue lace around the sides of the shoebox.

4. Cut two thin strips of the pink poster board into hearts, and bend them onto the two front corners of the shoebox. Glue them in place. Cut two little hearts from the red construction paper and glue them over the poster board hearts.

5. Sit the clay dolls on the clay bench and set them on the top of the shoebox, in the front.

6. Make a sign that says "Friends Forever" and glue it in front of the two clay dolls.

7. Glue the roses to the top of the shoebox, one on each side of the dolls.

8. Cut hearts from the red construction paper and glue in various places.

9. Glue friendship sayings near the roses.

Optional: If you don't have last year's box as described in direction #2, decorate a small shoebox lid with white construction paper and stickers. Make sure to make a slit.

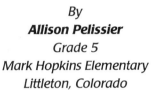

MY PINK GIRLFRIEND

By
Jessica Gallegos
Grade 3
Mark Hopkins Elementary
Littleton, Colorado

SUPPLIES

Dinner plate	Red permanent markers	Gift bag
Pencil	Red confetti	Ruler
Pink poster board	Stapler	Glue
Scissors	Two white pipe cleaners	Old doll shoes
Decorative items		

DIRECTIONS

1. Use a dinner plate to trace two circles onto the pink poster board for the head. Cut them out.

2. Make a face on one from the decorative items and permanent markers.

3. Stick confetti between the two circles for hair, and staple closed.

4. Shape pipe cleaners into arms and staple them to the sides of the bag.

5. Trace the ruler on the poster board twice. Cut out the shapes and bend back and forth like an accordion.

6. Glue the doll shoes onto the "accordion" legs, then glue the legs to the bottom of the gift bag.

7. Cut a rectangle out of the poster board the same size as the back of the gift bag. Glue it inside the bag for support.

8. Staple the head to the back of the bag.

9. Cut the handle off the bag.

10. Valentines can be dropped into the bag.

FRIENDS

SUPPLIES

Glue

White wrapping paper

Box

Permanent markers (assorted colors)

Scissors

4 inches Valentine fabric (or ribbon)

Fake flowers

Pom-poms

Heart stones

DIRECTIONS

1. Glue the white wrapping paper on the whole box.
2. Draw pictures of friends onto the front side of the box.
3. Make a slit above the friends for Valentine cards to be deposited. Cover the slit with a 4-inch piece of fabric, gluing it in place along the top.
4. Glue imitation flowers, pom-poms, and heart stones to the front corners.
5. Draw a design on the top of the box.

By
Kayla Schaecher
Grade 1
Mark Hopkins Elementary
Littleton, Colorado

LOVE & FRIENDSHIP BOXES

What items do you like to use when making your Valentine boxes?

"Stickers, pom-poms, and buttons."

Kelly Hill. Age 8

"Shiny paper, anything heart-shaped, heart doilies, and glitter."

Wilby Alley, Age 10

"Crayons, markers, and glue."
Alyssa Ripple, Age 7

SUPPLIES FOR LOVE & FRIENDSHIP BOXES

DIAMONDS ARE A GIRL'S BEST FRIEND

Tape

Small cardboard box

Pink wrapping paper

Glue gun

Scissors

Permanent markers

Imitation diamond studs

Imitation pearl strand

Imitation diamond ring

Four heart-stones

MISSISSIPPI RIVER LOVE BOAT

Large rectangular box with flip-top lid

Scissors

Stapler

Tape

Glue gun or craft glue

Medium square box

Small square box

Three toilet paper rolls

Lots of craft sticks broken in half

1/4" wooden dowel

5 x 16-inch poster board

Spray paint (any color)

Red permanent markers

Valentine heart stickers

Yarn or string (any color)

FRIENDS FOREVER

Large shoe box

Pink poster board

Glue

Last year's Valentine box lid

Scissors

White lace

Red construction paper

Clay dolls (handmade)

Clay bench (handmade)

1 x 3-inch white paper

Red permanent marker

Two silk roses (without stems)

Friendship sayings (from magazines, greeting cards, etc.)

Optional: Small shoe-box lid, white construction paper and Valentine heart stickers

MY PINK GIRLFRIEND

Dinner plate

Pencil

Pink poster board

Scissors

Decorative items

Red permanent markers

Red confetti

Stapler

Two white pipe cleaners

Gift bag

Ruler

Glue

Old doll shoes

FRIENDS

Glue

White wrapping paper

Box

Permanent markers (assorted colors)

Scissors

4 inches Valentine fabric (or ribbon)

Fake flowers

Pom-poms

Heart stones

Don't forget the camera and film.

ANIMAL BOXES

DALMATIAN VALENTINE BOX

SUPPLIES

Large round cardboard container with lid

White spray paint

Knife

Scissors

Large Styrofoam® cup

Glue gun

Pencil

Black construction paper

White construction paper

Small sponge

Black paint

Large moving eyes

Craft eyelashes

Black pom-pom

3 inches red yarn

Red craft foam (found in craft stores)

White fabric paint

Red ribbon

DIRECTIONS

1. Keep the lid on the container (body).

2. Spray the outside of the container with the white paint.

3. Cut a horizontal slit in the side of the container to slide Valentines through.

4. Cut about 2 inches off the top of the Styrofoam® cup, and glue to the container (neck). Save the rest of the cup.

5. Glue the Styrofoam® cup (head) onto the neck above the slit, as shown in the illustration.

6. Trace and cut one ear from the black construction paper. Trace and cut the following from the white construction paper: one ear, two arms, two legs, and one tail.

7. Glue all the legs and arms to the body, toward the slit. Glue on the tail and both ears. Bend the ears.

8. Cut the sponge into a heart shape and sponge black paint all over the dog for spots — on the body, head, neck, ears, arms, legs, and tail. Let dry.

9. Glue eyes and eyelashes to the sides of the head.

10. Glue the red yarn (mouth) and the pom-pom (nose) to the bottom of the cup.

11. Cut four medium-size hearts from the red craft foam, and glue one to each arm and leg at the "joints."

12. Cut a large heart from the craft foam and glue under the card slit.

13. Use the white fabric paint to decorate the five craft foam hearts. Write a Valentine saying on the large heart under the card slit.

14. Glue red ribbon around the neck and tie in a bow.

By
Holly Simpson
Grade 5
Mark Hopkins Elementary
Littleton, Colorado

By
Alex
Kindergarten
Mark Hopkins Elementary
Littleton, Colorado

ELEPHANT VALENTINE BOX

SUPPLIES

White or gray paper	Red construction paper	Black construction paper
Shoebox with lid	Tacky glue	Four small Valentine heart stickers
Tape	Pencil	
Scissors	Blue construction paper	

DIRECTIONS

1. Using the white or gray paper, separately wrap and tape the shoebox and lid.

2. Cut an elephant's mouth in the front of the box for Valentines to be deposited.

3. Cut floppy ears out of the red construction paper. Glue to the sides of the box.

4. Trace and cut the elephant's trunk out of the red construction paper using the pattern on this page. Fold the trunk along the dotted lines and glue the asterisks above the mouth.

5. Cut two round circles from the blue construction paper and glue on the box for eyes. Cut two pupils from the black construction paper and glue onto the eyes.

6. Cut two white shapes as shown in the illustration and glue over the black pupils. Add two Valentine heart stickers on top of those.

7. Add two Valentine heart stickers for the cheeks.

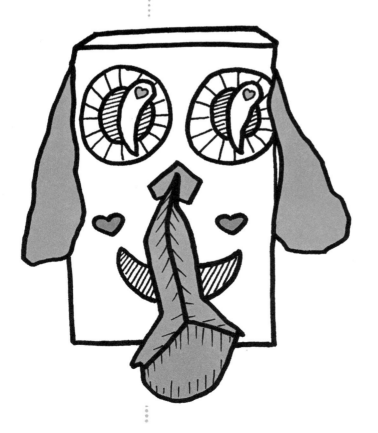

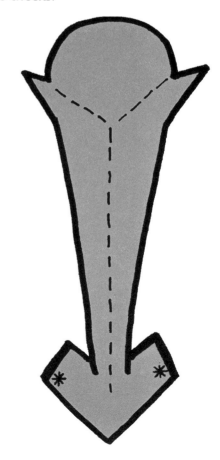

TEDDY BEAR VALENTINE BOX

SUPPLIES

Large empty cereal box	White or light-brown paint	Rocks
Ruler	Sponge	Small Valentine balloon on a stick
Pencil	Dark brown paint	
Scissors	Permanent markers	
Paint brush	Pink paint	

By
Katie Day
Grade 1
Mark Hopkins Elementary
Littleton, Colorado

DIRECTIONS

1. From the bottom of the cereal box, measure 3 to 4 inches up and draw a line around the front and sides of the box.

2. Cut off the front and sides of the cereal box down to the 3 to 4-inch line, leaving the back in one piece.

3. Draw the shape of a Teddy Bear's head and shoulders on the back inside of the box. Cut out without cutting the back off.

4. Cut the front of the box into paws so they touch, and tape together.

5. Paint all sides including the inside of the back of the box white or light brown. Sponge paint the bear's face, ears, and paws with the dark brown paint to look like fur, and let dry.

6. Draw on the face and paws with the permanent markers.

7. Cut a large heart out of the excess cardboard, paint pink, and let dry. Decorate the heart using the permanent markers. Tape it behind the paws.

8. Place a rock or two inside the box to help it stand upright. Stick the Valentine balloon in the box and tape in place.

9. Valentines are deposited in the box behind the large heart.

GIRAFFE

SUPPLIES

Paper-mache glue recipe (see next page)

Scissors

Shoebox with lid

Two toilet paper rolls

Masking tape

Paper towel roll

Newspaper and white paper (ripped into strips)

Drinking straw

Yellow poster paint

Brown poster paint

Paint brushes

Black permanent maker

Tacky glue

Black moving eyes (found at craft stores)

Eleven yellow pom-poms

By
Spencer Vore
Grade 1
Mark Hopkins Elementary
Littleton, Colorado

DIRECTIONS

1. Make the paper-mache glue and let cool.
2. Cut a large opening in the top of the shoebox for the Valentines to be deposited.
3. Cut both toilet paper rolls in half.
4. Use the masking tape to attach the toilet paper rolls to the bottom of the shoebox to form the legs.
5. Use the masking tape to attach the paper towel roll to the top of the shoebox, at one end, to form the neck.
6. Crumple up newspaper into a tight oval ball. Use masking tape to attach it on top of the neck to form the head.
7. Cut two small pieces from a straw. Bend them and tape onto the head to form the ears.
8. Use the remainder of the straw to make a tail, and tape it onto the shoebox opposite the head.
9. With your fingers, apply paper-mache glue to the body and layer on newspaper strips (or dip the paper in the glue and then apply). When the body is completely covered with newspaper, switch to white paper strips. This helps to see where one layer ends and another begins. Apply four layers, ending with white paper strips. (If you don't do this you will have to apply white latex paint as a primer to cover up the newsprint.)
10. Let the giraffe dry for two to three days.
11. Paint the entire giraffe yellow and let dry.
12. Paint brown spots on the body.
13. Draw nostrils and a mouth on the face using the black permanent marker.
14. Glue the moving eyes to the face.

15. Glue the pom-poms down the backside of the neck to make the mane.

Note: You'll need to make this box 2 to 3 days before using.

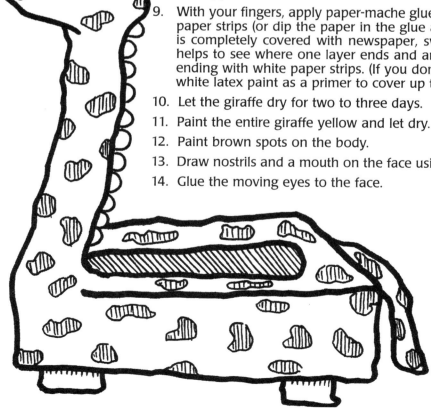

PAPER-MACHE GLUE SUPPLIES

6 cups water	Large pot
3 cups flour	Spoon

DIRECTIONS

1. Mix the water and flour together in the large pot.

2. Heat the mixture, either on the stove or in the microwave. Stir constantly (or occasionally in the microwave) until it has the consistency of thick cream.

3. Cool before using.

Roses are red
Violets are blue
This is for you
In case of the flu
Tammy Arcuri

Kim couldn't look
In her Valentine box
What if Jack had put in
A handful of rocks?
Karen Timm

By
Judi Krew
of "Judi Krew Creations"
with creative control by
Travis, Grade 1
Sauder Elementary
Canton, Ohio

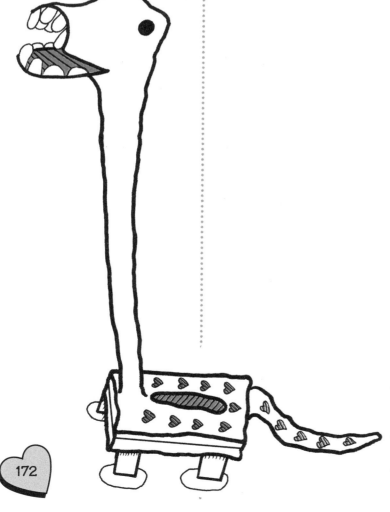

172

WORKING DINOSAUR BOX

SUPPLIES

Red fabric

Glue gun

Shoebox with lid

Green florist foil
(textured foil for
wrinkled skin
appearance)

Scissors

3 x 36-inch wrap-
ping paper tube

Tape

Four toilet paper
tubes

Four oval card-
board pieces
(about 2 inches
long)

Cardboard

Flat seashells

Pointed seashells

Red felt

Fishing line

Two clear-glass
pebbles

Metallic heart
stickers

DIRECTIONS

1. Line the inside of the box with red fabric.

2. Wrap and glue the shoebox and lid separately with the green florist foil. Cut out a section from the top of the box for Valentines to be deposited.

3. From the top of your 36-inch tube, cut down about 5 inches at the 4 and 8 o'clock positions. Bend the tube just below the cut to form the head.

4. Cover and glue the wrapping paper tube with the green florist foil.

5. Attach the bottom of the tube to the lid of the shoebox using glue and tape.

6. Glue each toilet paper tube to its own oval cardboard base, for the legs.

7. Cover and glue the legs with the green florist foil.

8. Glue the legs to the bottom of the shoebox.

9. Cut a dinosaur tail from the cardboard, long enough to drag on the ground. Cover and glue with the green florist foil. Glue the tail to the back of the shoebox.

10. Glue the seashells to the inside of the mouth, along the foil, for the teeth. Use flat shells for front, bottom teeth and pointed shells for upper, canine teeth.

11. Line the inside of the mouth with red fabric. Be careful not to knock the teeth out.

12. Cut a tongue from the red felt and glue one end in the back of the mouth.

13. Hook the fishing line down through the roof of the mouth, knotted above the snout and under the chin. Be sure to leave slack for movement. Bring the fishing line all the way down to the front side of the box and attach securely. Pull to make the mouth move and the shells "click" together for sound.

14. Form two pouches from the green florist foil. Glue a clear-glass pebble into each pouch to make the eyes.

15. Glue the eyes onto the sides of the dinosaur's head.

16. Decorate the shoebox and tail with metallic heart stickers.

TEDDY BEAR COTTON BALL BOX

SUPPLIES

Pencil
Cardboard
Scissors
Shoebox with lid
Tacky glue

Pink construction paper
Red construction paper
White lace

Cotton balls
Three brass buttons (eyes and nose)
Plastic hair bow

By
Brook Alessandrini
Grade 1
Sauder Elementary
Canton, Ohio

ANIMAL BOXES

DIRECTIONS

1. Draw the bear's head and arms on the cardboard.

2. Cut the bear-shape out.

3. Insert the bottom of the bear-shape into the open shoebox and glue.

4. Cut a slit in the top of the shoebox lid for the Valentines to be deposited. Fit the lid on the box, trimming around the bear-shape if necessary.

5. Cover and tape the box and lid with pink construction paper.

6. Cut two legs from the cardboard and glue them to the bottom of the shoebox.

7. Cut a few heart shapes from red construction paper and glue on the box.

8. Glue lace around the edge of the lid.

9. Glue cotton balls on the bear. Add a few extra cotton balls to the center of the face to make a snout.

10. Glue the buttons on the face, two buttons for the eyes and one for the nose.

11. Glue the plastic hair bow above the eyes.

173

THE VALENTINE CAT BOX

SUPPLIES

Hinged shoebox
Plain white paper
Tacky glue
Scissors

Red construction paper
Black construction paper

Two Valentine heart stickers
Assorted Valentine stickers

By
Matthew Cloyd
Grade 3
Laura Ingalls Wilder
Elementary
Littleton, Colorado

DIRECTIONS

1. Cover the box with plain white paper, making sure the lid can still open for Valentine cards to be deposited.

2. Cut two 3-inch tall triangles out of the red construction paper for the ears.

3. Glue the ears at an angle on the back corners of the box lid.

4. Cut two 2-inch ovals out of the black construction paper for the eyes. Glue onto the top of the box. Place a Valentine sticker on top of each black oval.

5. Cut two zigzag strips the length of your box out of the red construction paper for teeth.

6. Glue one strip of the teeth on the bottom of the front side of the box, points up. Glue the other strip just below the opening edge of the box, points down.

7. Decorate the box with lots of Valentine stickers!

174

HOPPY VALENTINE'S BOX

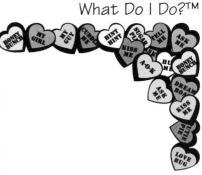

SUPPLIES

- Shoebox with lid
- 1/2 yard green fabric
- Stapler
- Tacky glue
- Scissors
- Green construction paper
- Three Valentine heart stickers
- Red construction paper
- Black permanent marker

By
Rachel Goold
Grade 1
Mark Hopkins Elementary
Littleton, Colorado

DIRECTIONS

1. Cover the shoebox, lid attached, with green fabric. Staple or glue in place.
2. Cut a mouth slit through the fabric and shoebox lid for Valentines to slide through. Bend the slit slightly upward so the tongue can slip in.
3. Cut eyes from the green construction paper and glue at the top edge of the box, sticking up. Place a heart sticker in the center of each eye.
4. Cut a tongue from the red construction paper and place a heart sticker on it. Using the black permanent marker, write "Hoppy Valentine's Day!" on the tongue. Glue to the inside roof of the mouth.
5. Cut two heart shapes from the red construction paper and glue to the box to make cheeks.

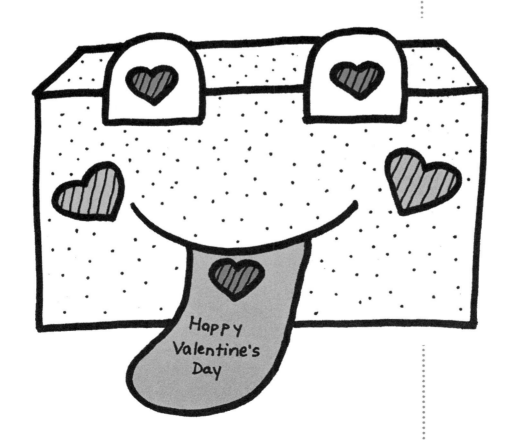

SUPPLIES FOR ANIMAL BOXES

DALMATIAN VALENTINE BOX

Large round cardboard container with lid

White spray paint

Knife

Scissors

Large Styrofoam® cup

Glue gun

Pencil

Black construction paper

White construction paper

Small sponge

Black paint

Large moving eyes

Craft eyelashes

Black pom-pom

3 inches red yarn

Red craft foam (found in craft stores)

White fabric paint

Red ribbon

ELEPHANT VALENTINE BOX

White or gray paper

Shoebox with lid

Tape

Scissors

Red construction paper

Tacky glue

Pencil

Blue construction paper

Black construction paper

Four small Valentine heart stickers

TEDDY BEAR VALENTINE BOX

Large empty cereal box

Ruler

Pencil

Scissors

Paint brush

White or light-brown paint

Sponge

Dark brown paint

Permanent markers

Pink paint

Rocks

Small Valentine balloon on a stick

GIRAFFE

Paper-mache glue recipe (see recipe on this page)

Scissors

Shoebox with lid

Two toilet paper rolls

Masking tape

Paper towel roll

Newspaper and white paper (ripped into strips)

Drinking straw

Yellow poster paint

Brown poster paint

Paint brushes

Black permanent maker

Tacky glue

Black moving eyes (found at craft stores)

Eleven yellow pom-poms

PAPER-MACHE GLUE RECIPE

6 cups water

3 cups flour

Large pot

Spoon

WORKING DINOSAUR BOX

Red fabric

Glue gun

Shoebox with lid

Green florist foil (textured foil for wrinkled skin appearance)

Scissors

3 x 36-inch wrapping paper tube

Tape

Four toilet paper tubes

Four oval cardboard pieces (about 2 inches long)

Cardboard

Flat seashells

Pointed seashells

Red felt

Fishing line

Two clear-glass pebbles

Metallic heart stickers

TEDDY BEAR COTTON BALL BOX

Pencil

Cardboard

Scissors

Shoebox with lid

Tacky glue

Pink construction paper

Red construction paper

White lace

Cotton balls

Three brass buttons (eyes and nose)

Plastic hair bow

THE VALENTINE CAT BOX

Hinged shoebox

Plain white paper

Tacky glue

Scissors

Red construction paper

Black construction paper

Two Valentine heart stickers

Assorted Valentine stickers

HOPPY VALENTINE'S BOX

Shoebox with lid

1/2 yard green fabric

Stapler

Tacky glue

Scissors

Green construction paper

Three Valentine heart stickers

Red construction paper

Black permanent marker

POST OFFICE BOXES

MICHELLE'S MAILBOX

SUPPLIES

Scissors

Red poster board

Shoebox (no lid)

Glue gun

Shoelace

Three paper fasteners

Fabric teddy bear

Pink construction paper

Black permanent marker

Small piece yellow construction paper

Brown permanent marker

12-inch wooden ruler

White paper

Red permanent marker

Three red pom-poms

Glitter

Tacky glue

By
Michelle Ripple
Grade 3
Mark Hopkins Elementary
Littleton, Colorado

DIRECTIONS

1. Cut the red poster board to curve over the shoebox and cover the two long sides. Glue in place.

2. Cut and fit another shape of the poster board to put on the front of the box. Add about 2 inches to the bottom portion before cutting. Fold in 2 inches and glue to the bottom front of the shoebox. Let dry for 10 minutes. Cut and fit another shape of the poster board to fit on the back of the box.

3. Attach a shoelace to the top of the box towards the front with a paper fastener.

4. Attach another paper fastener towards the top of the front flap. Loop the shoelace around this paper fastener to secure your door closed. Open the door to deposit Valentines.

5. Glue the fabric bear onto the front flap. Cut a medium-size heart from the pink construction paper. Using the black permanent marker, write "You're my Honey" on it. Glue to the front flap by the bear's mouth.

6. Cut a medium-size honey jar-shape from the yellow construction paper. Color the lid brown and write "Honey" on the front. Glue it next to the bear.

7. Cut a 1 x 14-inch strip from the extra poster board. Using the same poster board, cut a large heart. Cut a heart-shape in its center. Glue the heart at the end of the strip for the mailbox flag.

8. Glue the wooden ruler onto the back of the flag strip leaving 2 inches of the flag strip to attach to the mailbox.

9. Cover the flag strip with white paper and draw red hearts on it.

10. Attach the extra 2 inches of the flag to the box using a paper fastener. This will let you raise or lower the flag.

11. Glue red pom-poms to the top of the box.

12. Draw hearts on the sides of the box and glue on glitter with tacky glue.

177

VALENTINE'S CASTLE MAILBOX

SUPPLIES

Scissors

Two paper towel tubes

Paint brushes (thin and thick)

Red acrylic paint

Empty pizza box

Green acrylic paint

8½ x 11-inch white construction paper

Black permanent marker

Tacky glue

Plastic wrap

Medium-size box with flaps (8 x 6 x 6½ inches)

Tape

8½ x 11-inch red construction paper

White acrylic paint

Black acrylic paint

Blue acrylic paint

8½ x 11-inch brown construction paper

By
Taylor Craver
Grade 3
Laura Ingalls Wilder
Elementary
Littleton, Colorado

DIRECTIONS

1. Cut notches in one end of each paper towel tube to resemble tops of castle towers.

2. Paint the outside of the towers, and the top, sides, and flaps of the box red.

3. Paint the pizza box green and set aside.

4. Cut out two 4½ x 9½-inch rectangles from white construction paper. These will become the front door.

5. Keeping them together, fold both in half width-wise, being sure to make a center crease. Open them back up, and lay flat.

6. Fold the ends into the center crease to make two doors that resemble French doors.

7. Keeping the doors closed, use the black permanent marker to draw a large heart that fills the front of the two doors. The point should start at the bottom of the center crease and the top should also come to a "V" at the center crease.

8. Cut out only the top of the doors along the heart pattern, through both pieces of paper.

9. Draw two matching heart-shaped windows on the top half of each door. Cut out the windows.

10. Glue small squares of plastic wrap inside the windows for glass.

11. Open the French doors and paint people, one behind each door so that when the doors are closed they are peeking out of the windows. Add a Valentine saying inside the doors using the black permanent marker. Glue the French doors to the front of the box.

12. Cut a triangle in both side flaps of the box, so that the front and back flaps can fold inward to make a pointed roof on your castle. Be sure to leave an opening for your Valentine cards to be deposited.

13. Tape the roof together on the inside of the box.

14. Cut two strips of red construction paper 2 inches wide by the length of the box. Fold both papers in half lengthwise, open up to lay flat, and cut notches in the top half of each paper to match the tops of the towers.

15. Glue them to the top edge of the box at the front and back of the castle.

16. Glue the towers to the side of the castle.

17. Paint white lines on all sides of the castle and towers to resemble bricks. Paint black lines on the roof to resemble shingles, and let dry.

18. Glue the castle onto the center of the pizza box and paint a moat around the outside of the castle using blue paint. Let dry. Be sure to leave some green to resemble land around your moat!

19. Make small doors and windows on the towers using black paint.

20. From the brown construction paper, cut a rectangle the same width as the door, and long enough to extend over the moat to the grass. This will become the drawbridge.

21. Make lines on the drawbridge to resemble wood markings and boards, using the black permanent marker. Glue the drawbridge to the front of the door and across the moat.

Do you enjoy making Valentine boxes? Why?

"Yes, it's fun and interesting but we never get to do it, we make folders and tape them to the back of our chairs."
Priscilla Ripple, Age 7

"Yes, because it gives you a chance to be creative."
Anonymous

POST OFFICE BOXES

By
Wilhelminia Ripple
Littleton, Colorado

VALENTINE MAIL TRUCK

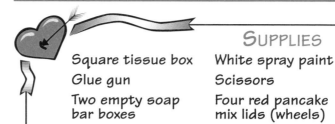

SUPPLIES

Square tissue box	White spray paint	Black permanent marker
Glue gun	Scissors	
Two empty soap bar boxes	Four red pancake mix lids (wheels)	

DIRECTIONS

1. Turn the tissue box on its side.

2. Glue two empty soapboxes at the opening of the tissue box, one in front of the other, to make the front of the truck.

3. Spray paint all the boxes white and let dry.

4. Cut out a door on the left side of the truck, leaving one side attached for the hinged side. This is where Valentines are deposited.

5. Glue the pancake mix lids, with the inside of the lids facing outward, to the truck for the wheels. Make sure the front wheels are glued to the soap-boxes.

6. Draw hubcaps on the inside of the lids with the permanent marker.

7. Use the permanent marker to write "Valentine Mail Truck" on the sides of your truck. Add a heart design next to the words.

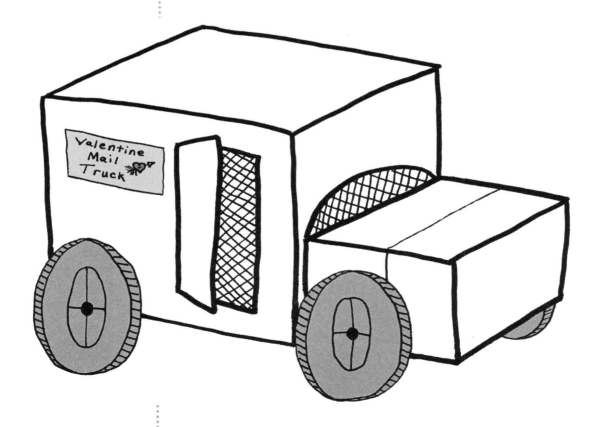

ROBOT DELIVERY BOX

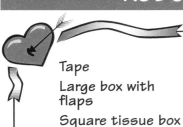

SUPPLIES

Tape

Large box with flaps

Square tissue box

Pencil

Scissors

Two toilet paper rolls

Aluminum foil

Two plastic spoons

Glue

Two coffee stir sticks

Valentine heart stickers (two small, two medium, two large)

White paper

Black permanent marker

By
Erin Johnson and her dad
Littleton, Colorado
February, 1992

DIRECTIONS

1. Tape up the large box so the flaps are closed.

2. Place the tissue box on the center top of the large box. Trace around the tissue box, and cut out the square.

3. Also, cut the bottom off of the tissue box.

4. Cut a mouth in the tissue box. This is where you will deposit Valentines. They will drop into the larger box.

5. Match up the tissue box with the hole in the large box. Tape in place.

6. Cut the toilet paper rolls in half at an angle and tape together to make elbows (as shown in the illustration). Tape the arms to the large box.

7. Cover both boxes and arms with foil. Re-slit the mouth.

8. Break the handles off the spoons.

9. Cover one spoon handle in foil. This will become the nose.

10. Cover the bowl part of both spoons with foil. These will become the eyes.

11. Glue the nose and eyes in place. Glue the spoon eyes to the face so they "bulge" out.

12. Glue on the coffee stir sticks (antennas) in place and stick a medium-size heart sticker on each end.

13. Stick a small heart sticker onto each spoon eye.

14. Cut out a heart shape from the white paper and write "Robby the Robot" on it.

15. Add three large heart stickers to the body for the buttons.

SUPPLIES FOR POST OFFICE BOXES

MICHELLE'S MAILBOX

Scissors

Red poster board

Shoebox (no lid)

Glue gun

Shoelace

Three paper fasteners

Fabric teddy bear

Pink construction paper

Black permanent marker

Small piece yellow construction paper

Brown permanent marker

12-inch wooden ruler

White paper

Red permanent marker

Three red pom-poms

Glitter

Tacky glue

VALENTINE'S CASTLE MAILBOX

Scissors

Two paper towel tubes

Paint brushes (thin and thick)

Red acrylic paint

Empty pizza box

Green acrylic paint

8½ x 11-inch white construction paper

Black permanent marker

Tacky glue

Plastic wrap

Medium-size box with flaps
(8 x 6 x 6½ inches)

Tape

8½ x 11-inch red construction paper

White acrylic paint

Black acrylic paint

Blue acrylic paint

8½ x 11-inch brown construction paper

VALENTINE MAIL TRUCK

Square tissue box

Glue gun

Two empty soap bar boxes

White spray paint

Scissors

Four red pancake mix lids (wheels)

Black permanent marker

ROBOT DELIVERY BOX

Tape

Large box with flaps

Square tissue box

Pencil

Scissors

Two toilet paper rolls

Aluminum foil

Two plastic spoons

Glue

Two coffee stir sticks

Valentine heart stickers (two small, two medium, two large)

White paper

Black permanent marker

FEBRUARY & PRESIDENTS' BOXES

GEORGE WASHINGTON VALENTINE BOX

SUPPLIES

Empty cereal box	Scissors	Blue construction paper
Peach construction paper	Pencil	Stapler
Tacky glue	8 inches blue ribbon	
White construction paper	Pink colored pencil	
	Moving eyes	

By
Thomas Christiansen
Kindergarten
Mark Hopkins Elementary
Littleton, Colorado

DIRECTIONS

1. Cover the front of the box with peach construction paper and glue down.

2. Cover all the sides with white construction paper.

3. Cut four strips of white construction paper, the same width as the narrow sides of the cereal box, and curl by rolling on a pencil. This will become the hair.

4. Glue two strips on each side of the box at the top, with one just above the other. These will make George Washington's side curls.

5. Make the back ponytail the same way by taking a sheet of construction paper the same size as the back of the box. Cut 1/2-inch sections lengthwise, stopping 1 inch from the top of the paper. Curl the strips on a pencil, but not as tightly as the side curls.

6. Glue the back ponytail to the top of the box back. Loosely "tie" the hair into a ponytail with ribbon.

7. Cut a large open mouth in a smile shape on the front of the box for the Valentines to be deposited.

8. Draw lips around the mouth with the pink colored pencil.

9. Glue the moving eyes to the top front of the box.

10. Draw a nose using the pink colored pencil.

11. To make George Washington's hat, cut one piece of blue construction paper lengthwise into thirds.

12. Round off all the corners.

13. Staple all three lengths together to make a three-sided hat.

14. Glue or staple onto George Washington's head.

ABRAHAM LINCOLN VALENTINE BOX

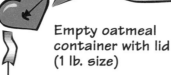

By
Tyler Sales
Grade 4
John Christiansen
Grade 5
Mark Hopkins Elementary
Littleton, Colorado

SUPPLIES

Empty oatmeal container with lid (1 lb. size)	Five pieces of black construction paper	Scissors
		Black permanent marker
Peach construction paper	Pencil	Red permanent marker
Glue gun	Black poster board	

DIRECTIONS

1. Cover the bottom one-third of the carton with peach construction paper and glue.

2. Cover the top two-thirds of the carton with black construction paper. Also, cover the top of the carton with black construction paper, including the lid.

3. Trace a circle onto the black poster board using the oatmeal carton. Draw another circle around the first one, 1½ inches larger. Cut the center circle out, then cut around the outer circle. This will be the hat brim.

4. Slide the hat brim onto the carton and glue it in place where the black and peach paper meet.

5. To make Lincoln's beard, cut three pieces of black construction paper in U-shapes, each large enough to go halfway around the carton.

6. Feather cut the outside edges for whiskers.

7. Fluff the whiskers with your fingers.

8. Stagger and glue the unfeathered edges of the whiskers around the face from hat brim to hat brim. Make the bottom edge of the whiskers even with the bottom of the carton.

9. Using a black permanent marker, draw eyes below the hat brim. Using a red permanent marker, draw a mouth under the beard.

10. Cut a large triangle from the peach construction paper. Fold in half and glue above the beard for a nose.

11. Cut a slit in the top of the carton to deposit the Valentines.

184

FIRECRACKER VALENTINE BOX

SUPPLIES

Empty oatmeal container (3 lb. size)

Red or black felt

Glue gun

Yellow felt

Scissors

Flower spikes that look like an explosion (yellow and pearl white work well)

Metallic heart and star stickers

Piece of wood for container to stand on

Green fabric to cover wood

Empty match book

6 to 8 inches of rope

Spray adhesive

Gold glitter

Ribbon to go around lid of oatmeal container

By
Nathan Finneman
Grade 3
Laura Ingalls Wilder Elementary
Littleton, Colorado

DIRECTIONS

1. Wrap the oatmeal carton with red or black felt, and glue.

2. Wrap the lid of the oatmeal carton with yellow felt, and glue. Cut an opening in the lid wide enough and long enough for Valentines to slide through.

3. Poke holes into the lid and glue in the spikes. They will look like a firecracker with sparks flying.

4. Put metallic heart and star stickers on the tips of the spikes. Put the stickers together on both sides of spikes to secure.

5. Put the sticker backing around the bottom of the firecracker to add to the design. It will stay in place because of its stickiness.

6. Cover the wood base with green fabric to look like grass. Glue down.

7. Glue the firecracker to the fabric-covered wood. Glue a matchbook on the wood base. Put heart stickers on the matchbook.

8. Spray the rope with spray adhesive and sprinkle on gold glitter to make it look lit.

9. Glue the rope to the bottom of the firecracker so it looks like a lit fuse.

10. Glue ribbon around the top of the lid. Now you have a unique Firecracker Valentine Box.

185

By
Scott Heldt
Grade 3
Laura Ingalls Wilder
Elementary
Littleton, Colorado

SCOTT'S VALENTINE ROBOT

SUPPLIES

Tape	Three toilet paper rolls	Assorted candy for face and decorations
Small shoe box	Glue gun	
Square jewelry box	Gray spray paint	Black permanent marker
Scissors		

DIRECTIONS

1. Tape both boxes closed, being careful to cover all seams.
2. Cut a section from the center of the shoebox lid for the Valentine cards to be deposited. Stand the box on its short side.
3. Cut one toilet paper roll in half and glue the halves on the bottom of the box for the legs.
4. Glue the other toilet paper rolls, one to each side of the box, for the arms.
5. Glue the jewelry box on its side to the top of the shoebox to form the head.
6. Spray paint the entire robot, and let dry.
7. Glue candy on the small box to make a face. Add additional candy to the body if desired.
8. Personalize the box with your name, following it with the word "Robot."

Scott's Robot

186

WADE'S KISS VALENTINE BOX

SUPPLIES

Round-shaped basket with handle

Clear plastic wrap

Aluminum foil

Scissors

7-inch strip white paper

Black permanent marker

Stapler

DIRECTIONS

1. Cover the basket with clear plastic wrap to make it a bit more stable.

2. Wrap the basket with aluminum foil, leaving enough foil to form a kiss tip. Twist the foil and staple.

3. Cut a slit through the foil and plastic wrap for Valentines to be deposited.

4. Flag-tip one end of the paper. Then personalize it with your name and the word "Kiss."

5. Hang the paper from the top of the kiss to hide the Valentine slit. Staple the paper to the foil.

By
Wade Brown
Grade 3
Laura Ingalls Wilder Elementary Littleton, Colorado

SUPPLIES FOR FEBRUARY & PRESIDENTS' BOXES

GEORGE WASHINGTON VALENTINE BOX

Empty cereal box

Peach construction paper

Tacky glue

White construction paper

Scissors

Pencil

8 inches blue ribbon

Pink colored pencil

Moving eyes

Blue construction paper

Stapler

ABRAHAM LINCOLN VALENTINE BOX

Empty oatmeal container with lid (1 lb. size)

Peach construction paper

Glue gun

Five pieces of black construction paper

Pencil

Black poster board

Scissors

Black permanent marker

Red permanent marker

FIRECRACKER VALENTINE BOX

Empty oatmeal container (3 lb. size)

Red or black felt

Glue gun

Yellow felt

Scissors

Flower spikes that look like an explosion (yellow and pearl white work well)

Metallic heart and star stickers

Piece of wood for container to stand on

Green fabric to cover wood

Empty match book

6 to 8 inches of rope

Spray adhesive

Gold glitter

Ribbon to go around lid of oatmeal container

SCOTT'S VALENTINE ROBOT

Tape

Small shoe box

Square jewelry box

Scissors

Three toilet paper rolls

Glue gun

Gray spray paint

Assorted candy for face and decorations

Black permanent marker

WADE'S KISS VALENTINE BOX

Round-shaped basket with handle

Clear plastic wrap

Aluminum foil

Scissors

7-inch strip white paper

Black permanent marker

Stapler

Roses are Red,
Violets are Blue,
I trust this book,
Will work well for you.

Till next time
Willie

ORDER FORM

Become an expert the easy way!
Order from the What Do I Do?™ series.
CALL OUR TOLL FREE HOTLINE TO ORDER TODAY AT
1-888-738-1733

Oakbrook Publishing House
P.O. Box 2463
Littleton, CO 80161-2463
Phone: (303) 738-1733
Fax: (303) 797-1995
Website: http://www.whatdoidobooks.com

Mail to

Name: _____

Address: _____

City, State & Zip Code: _____ Phone: (____) _____

Order 2 books and get a 10% discount or order 3 or more books and get a 10% discount and free shipping.

Book Title	Quantity	Price	Total
Halloween School Parties...What Do I Do?™ ISBN: 0-9649939-8-8	_____	$19.95 ea.	$_____
Valentine School Parties...What Do I Do?™ ISBN: 0-9649939-9-6	_____	$19.95 ea	$_____
Valentine Boxes...What Do I Do?™ ISBN: 0-9649939-3-7	_____	$12.95 ea.	$_____
Teacher's Gifts...What Do I Do?™ (call for information)		Subtotal	$_____
		Shipping & Handling (see below)	$_____
Christmas School Parties...What Do I Do?™ (call for information)		Colorado Res. Add 3.8% sales tax	$_____
		Discount	$_____
		Total	$_____

100% fully guaranteed on all orders

_____ Check or Money Order payable to: Oakbrook Publishing House

_____ Credit card   Visa _____   Master Card _____   Discover _____

Card Number _____ Exp. Date _____

Signature_____

Canadian orders must be accompanied by a postal money order in U.S. funds.
Shipping and Handling charges are:
1st class $3.50, 4th class $2.25 (Allow 7-10 days for 4th class mail), additional books add $1.00 each.

COMING SOON:
Teacher's Gifts...What Do I Do?™
Christmas School Parties...What Do I Do?™